LIVING LANDSCAPES

CREATIVE VISIONS OF THE WILD

First published 2009 by Argentum an imprint of Aurum Press Ltd,
7 Greenland Street, London NW1 0ND.

A catalogue record for this book is available from the British Library.

ISBN 978 1 902538 56 3

Designed by Eddie Ephraums.

Printed in Singapore.

Previous page:
Roe buck at sunset

Opposite page:
King penguin on beach

LIVING LANDSCAPES

CREATIVE VISIONS OF THE WILD

Andy Rouse

ARGENTUM

CONTENTS

Opposite page:
Kingfisher in frost

INTRODUCTION

Welcome to *Living Landscapes*, a book that will hopefully fire your imagination by helping you to look at the natural world with fresh eyes. *Living Landscapes* picks up from where my previous book, *Concepts of Nature*, left off. Whilst *Concepts of Nature* concentrated on my use of light, *Living Landscapes* looks at the natural world from a more creative perspective where light is just one of many factors. The visual story I tell in *Living Landscapes* is very different from what you may regard as the norm for nature books. In fact, the pictures in this book are deliberately meant to challenge rather than to conform. In posing this challenge, I am not trying to be controversial. I am just trying to show how one photographer's work continues to grow and expand its horizons. You should not consider this book as a finished piece of work. Instead it is very much a work in progress, showing the images that I have made to date and perhaps setting the future direction for much of my work.

So what defines a Living Landscape? In my view, it is simply an image that expresses the relationship between a habitat and the species that exist within it. Any Living Landscape image must include an element of both and in order to take them I have had to step back from my usual 'shoot from the hip' style of photography to combine these two elements. Sometimes I will decide that the story is best told in a wide-angle view to show a subject in the context of the habitat in which it lives. Usually I do this if the light is exceptional or if there is moody weather. At other times, I may decide to take an abstract which provides no clues about the subject's scale; for example, the viewer may be unable to determine whether the subject is 2 feet away or 2000. I love to do this to trigger the viewer's imagination and bring out the wonderful patterns in nature. Then there is the experimental work where I am letting my creativity overrule technical considerations; usually I do this in order to show the elegance of motion. Not everyone likes this kind of photography, but that is cool – we are all different and one person's art may be another person's nightmare.

Above all, this is a book that comes straight from my animal-hugger heart. I want to show the natural world at its best, because I am an animal-lover and conservationist first and foremost; the photographer within me plays a secondary role. I live to spend time with wildlife, to experience the thrill of looking into wild eyes or seeing the daily struggle for existence played out before me. I take pictures which I hope will inspire others to help protect this wonderful planet that we all live on. My personal wish for *Living Landscapes* is that it will inspire you to look deeper into the amazing natural world around us. Only by appreciating what we already have now can we ever hope to save it to inspire generations to come.

Opposite page:
Lioness on a windy day

Following pages (8-9):
King penguins on beach

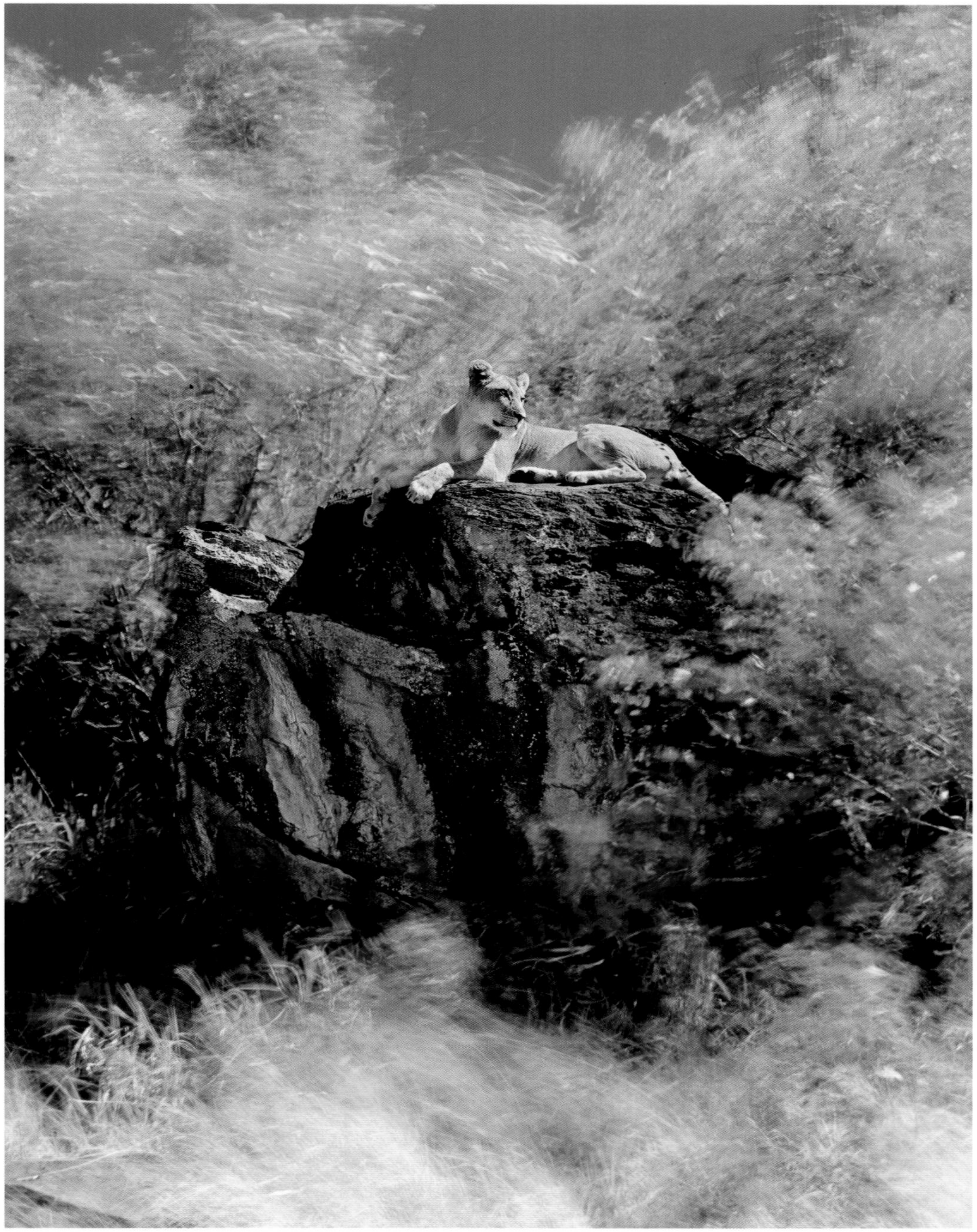

IN CONVERSATION

… WITH EDDIE EPHRAUMS

Living Landscapes is the second book I have worked on with Andy. Right now we're in a café, taking a break from page layouts (figuring out where each image should go and how it fits in with the overall narrative). We are here to discuss where we are at with the book and, at the same time, to step back from it and simply watch the world go by. We spend a fair amount of time in cafés. They seem to work well for our discussions – a natural environment in which to talk and, therefore, to do an interview, a place where we can simply be ourselves.

On reflection, a café-interview also parallels one of Andy's desires for *Living Landscapes*: to get away from stereotypical portraits and experience the subject in a more natural way, as an integral part of the habitat and, more challengingly in this book, *as* the habitat – just as it *is* the people that make up a café, not simply the building.

Andy speaks openly about himself and his work. In fact, anyone who has been to one of his lectures would say he is supremely confident, that he doesn't need a café environment to help him talk. True, perhaps…

Confidence and discipline

Like many artists, I would say his confidence is not innate, rather it is fuelled by a commitment: whatever the situation, whether it be in the wild, photographing animals, or being interviewed in a café, I suspect he always tries his best at the task in hand. I've met other highly successful photographers for whom this is also true. None are reasonable people, who just do the sensible thing, giving up when hope is lost, only to witness the long-awaited subject appear just after the camera has been packed away.

'Some people have a preconceived idea of what it takes to be a wildlife photographer and how easy it must be,' he says. 'But, when I take fellow photographers on location with me, I say, "You mustn't copy me, you mustn't stand next to me and take the same images. Instead, take the pictures you are happy with." I try to give them the confidence to do that. What photographers also need to realize is that the way other photographers do things is neither better nor necessarily right; instead they should find their own way. I suggest that they learn to talk about their photographs and put them into competitions. I tell them, "I take as many rubbish pictures as you

Opposite page:
Lioness – if looks could kill

do, the difference is that I don't miss good ones!" I focus; I concentrate; I have an affinity with animals – I always have – and I have good fieldcraft. I know when a bird might be about to take off or when an animal is showing the signs that tell me it's hacked off with me.'

A trip to Antarctica on the Royal Navy's HMS *Endurance* helped to put 'some discipline' into Andy's life. 'Normally, I'm in control of everything, for example on safari, but on *Endurance* I had to get used to justifying what I was doing, accepting it when an idea got turned down and making the most of whatever opportunities were offered to me. I couldn't wait until the light was right, because they wouldn't wait, the ship had other priorities. It taught me to invent, to work positively when a compromise had to be made.'

Self-perception
His first trip to the Falklands changed Andy's perception of what he could do. It was not a military trip, 'My time was my own. I learned to calm down, to take things slowly and watch events as they unfolded. Before, as a wildlife photographer, I had shot from the hip; this time I began to wait for things to happen; for example, at an albatross colony the birds forgot I existed. I even fell asleep amongst them. This more relaxed approach helps me take better pictures – and sometimes I'm happy to take none at all. My life is primarily about animals, not about photography. I used to be wary of saying that, because photography can be such a technology- as opposed to subject-dominated occupation.

'If I couldn't be a wildlife photographer, would I still watch wildlife? Absolutely! Ask a wedding photographer if they would still go to weddings if they couldn't photograph them. I wonder how many would say yes, that they would still go. It's about having a passion for something, not just for the end-result of getting a picture or making money. You've got to be happy with yourself and with the reason you do what you do. In the past I took pictures for stock. The first time I photographed tigers it was for stock. This last time, I just wanted to see the tigers. At lectures, I talk about animals more than about photography. People are often surprised by this, but I say photography is just a series of numbers. For 99% of the time I'm not taking pictures, I'm watching animals and by doing that (rather than being on my mobile phone or ipod) I'm taking better pictures. If I've been there for some time, the animal is much more likely to behave naturally.'

A love of animals
Andy's love of animals can be traced back to when he was a child, growing up in an urban environment. 'David Attenborough was responsible for taking me around the world, in a way that I now want to do with my own pictures. He has

Great grey owl chick
*A very oblique angle that I achieved by lying on the ground. The
great grey owl chick had just left the nest and I wanted to show
it in the context of the forest habitat that it calls home. I love the
converging lines of the trees and the warping effect of a wide-
angle lens; the expression on the face of the owl is probably one
of sheer confusion!*

Previous page:
Bengal tiger in temple

been an amazing influence on millions of people.' But it wasn't always the wildlife
that came first. Before being a wildlife photographer Andy was in computer
sales and technical marketing. 'There was a win-at-all-costs business ethic. It
took me quite a few years to get that out of my system. During the first half of
my photographic career, that approach did its best to destroy things. Had I not
changed I would not have produced *Concepts of Nature* or *Living Landscapes*. It
makes me shudder to think back to when I wanted to be number one. There is no
number one; we're all good at different things. I'm good at marketing, but all I want
to do is wildlife. There's nothing else I could do now.'

That said, he needs to have a business head for what he does. 'Picture sales
finance my trips, although when I'm away for a month I can't answer emails and
I don't worry about missing a sale. This leaves me free to get on with it. I'm good
at evaluating myself and what's going on. I worked out what wasn't working
(spending too much time worrying about being number one, competing with big
agencies and trying to do the work of ten people). I don't have any assistants,
I don't want to drive a Ferrari (although I did!). It's about trying to get a good
balance between work and what's outside it. Listening to music, being with
the people I care about and being relaxed with them (and not talking about
photography). The more relaxed I am the better I am – and continue to become.
When I come back from a trip, I can put the camera down and have no desire to
use it for a month; I'm not obsessed with cameras like some photographers – but
with animals, yes.'

On photography
Andy says he hates buying new equipment. 'I can only shoot with one camera and
one lens at a time. Having extra gear affects my judgment. I like having equipment
I'm familiar with. But, when I need to buy something I will buy the best technology
to help me and my photography.'

How might photography change over the coming years? 'It will get more creative.
All manner of things have been photographed to death, so we're seeing repetitive
images of ever more familiar subjects. Photographers will be forced to take
chances to generate better work. Look at photographic competitions: the standard
is getting higher; the pictures that took time and commitment are winning.

'A lot of people say that digital has lowered the standard of photography. It may
have done so initially, because it was "too easy", but it's still as difficult to be
creative. Digital has freed me up, although I don't use live view; it's not good
enough yet, but it can be useful for lying down, photographing at a low angle. I
could use it to trigger my camera from a laptop, but I like to be there, to experience

the moment. That's why I don't like camera-trap photography, because I'm not there to witness the event and take the image.

'I made the switch to digital purely because it is a better tool than the one I was using. Now, creatively, because of high ISO settings, I can get very good results at ISO 1000-2000, and I can continue shooting into low light when some animals start to become active. I don't have to worry about the ISO any more, unlike with film. Now I just look at the shutter speed, or what aperture I need to control the depth of field. A shot I have of two tigers fighting was made at ISO 4000. It suits my style of photography, which is very much hand-held. Tripods are for beardies! I like the freedom of shooting hand-held; I'm not as creative when I work with a tripod. I generate my best work when I've got my camera around my neck. And, I've taken good pictures on a compact. Too much time and effort is devoted to discussing what camera and what systems people use. Many people have a better kit than me. A lot of pros don't always have the best kit.'

And retouching images? 'I think it's fine as long as it is a faithful rendition of what I saw, and the constituent parts of the image are in the same relation to each other. If we change the constituent parts then that falls into the dodgy area of image manipulation. We mustn't then say it's a wildlife image, but a composite art image.'

Do I consider my work as art? 'My photography is a work in progress, professionally, I'm developing all the time. I'm not entirely sure where it is headed. I'm not naturally an artistic person; my pictures are what I feel at the time. They reflect my emotions. What defines artistic? Something that is not a straight image, that takes a more creative approach, that changes what you are trying to say about what you saw through the viewfinder. I want to enhance what I see by applying some creative thinking to it, by trying to stamp my personality on an image; but I'm not always aiming to create something that isn't there. I evaluate each situation. Sometimes it might a be a straight animal head shot, other times I aim to be creative. It's always a case of picking the right "tool" for the job.

'About the pictures in the book? They are not like a finished project; they are my first faltering foray into showing this kind of work. I'm still learning – still at the beginning. Some pictures may be a bit naive, or a bit experimental, and I know I may receive criticism from the establishment, but in order to stay ahead you simply have to try different things.'

On conservation
'Let's be honest, in the world of conservation I'm inconsequential, I don't have the knowledge, but I can help with the media, albeit in a very small way. A lot of people

Cheetahs and rainbow
It had been a grim cloudy day and I had spent most of it reading a book whilst waiting for the light to come. To make it worse a late afternoon thunderstorm had appeared from nowhere and had deluged the plains. The cheetahs I had spent the day with were soaked to the bone and huddled up together on a mound. Just as I thought my luck was out, the last rays of the setting sun broke through the clouds and cast a beautiful glow across the plains. The cheetahs lit up and a rainbow formed behind, just rewards for a long wait.

ask how they can help to conserve tigers, for example. You can give money, but the best way is to ensure the animals have a value to the local economy by going out there and staying in local hotels and supporting the local tourist industry, doing tourist-type things when you are there. If we do this there is less incentive for locals to poach them. For example, visitors have very limited access to tiger game reserves. The animals rule the roost. Animal tourism encourages the local government to protect them; they want tourism. It appeals to every government's need for foreign currency. Also, I try to connect with local people when I'm out there. We need to get to know other cultures. Conflict exists in the world because we don't understand other people; also we need to present a positive image of our own culture, so they have a good impression of us.

'Conserving animals is also about protecting the landscape, the ecosytem and the habitat. It's fine to protect the animals, but what about the prey species? It needs an awful lot of animals to support just one tiger, but prey species are often food for local populations, too. There may be a conflict between man's needs and those of the animals. The world won't stop what it does; the population will keep growing, so we just have to manage wildlife havens whatever the cost. The World Land Trust buys up tracts of land and gives them to local people to protect. One of my dreams is to own a piece of woodland or an area of marshland with a pond and hedgerows, and protect it but not try to manage it. Until then, I'm happy to be inspired watching a robin for an hour in a back garden, or listening to a song thrush – whose call is as beautiful as that of any other bird on the planet. We overlook the wildlife that surrounds us, and I'm as guilty as anyone, although I do photograph a lot of British wildlife.'

At this point in the conversation the battery on my laptop is about to pack up. There is much else we could talk about, but it's time to head back and continue the page layouts of *Living Landscapes*. I wonder how different this conversation would have been had we stayed in and had our coffee at Andy's place? It's like wildlife photography, I suppose. Not much is likely to happen unless you get out there.

Starling murmuration

Over the following few pages you will see a mini portfolio of my most recent work completed just before this book went to press. The images show the incredible gathering of starlings in winter, called a "murmuration", and are Living Landscapes of the purest form.

Starling ballet 1
I always try to look for patterns when working with the starlings;
here I can see a goose and a pig, what can you see?

Starling ballet 2

It is simply amazing that one of the greatest spectacles in the natural world happens right on my doorstep. Every night during the middle of winter, tens of thousands of common starlings return en masse to their overnight roost. Sometimes they go straight down into the roost, but on other nights they perform a spectacular aerial ballet. They wheel around chattering to each other and growing in numbers every second. One minute the sky is full of starlings from horizon to horizon, then suddenly, they bunch up and form incredible shapes. One reason for this is that predators such as sparrowhawks and peregrine falcons are chasing them.

Starling shapes

More incredible shapes and I just look at these images in awe but also with sadness, as the common starling is suffering a decline due to changes in the agricultural and urban environments. Organizations like the RSPB and WWT (Wildfowl & Wetlands Trust) are working to highlight the decline but my big worry is that for several nights at the peak of the murmuration, there were only two people watching this spectacle. It is well known locally, yet no parents had brought their children to see this astonishing display and there were no school trips. It is such a sad commentary on modern life that children are not exposed to these wonders and I am seriously worried for the future of the starling. If kids do not know that starlings do this, then what hope do we have of saving the starlings? So I would say to anyone reading this who has small children, please find out where your local roost is and take your kids to see it. Trust me, they will love it and your child may grow up to be the one that really makes a difference. Someone has to.

HABITAT

AT ONE WITH NATURE

If *Concepts of Nature* illustrated one thing, it was that I was mature enough to admit my photography was a bit tired and needed to evolve. I did not make these changes for commercial reasons, despite what some cynics have implied, as much of the imagery I shoot now is financial suicide! No, the real reason for change was the best one. I wanted to let my creative side really express itself and it was simply something I felt I had to do. Yes, I have made mistakes along the way and yes, it has been a steep learning curve, but finally I feel that I am able to share my passion for the natural world and inspire others to do the same. That is what *Living Landscapes* is intended to show and I hope that you can see this passion expressed in the portfolio that follows.

These pictures are not just portraits of wildlife, but images that show fragments of ecosystems and reveal the relationship between the habitat and the wildlife that fights for survival within it. For me, these images make a far better case for conservation than any beautiful close-up and I now rarely take a shot that does not include some element of the subject's habitat. As you will know, this hasn't always been the case with me. I still get incredibly frustrated with myself when I think of all the glorious opportunities I missed in the past by using a huge lens. In contrast, all of these images are taken with the shorter lenses that most photographers have in their kit bag. It is not the gear that counts in these instances but the perception and the desire to show something different. It is the landscape and the light within it that form the essential elements of the image. In some images the wildlife occupies such a small part of the picture that it is difficult to identify what it actually is. However, in these cases it is the power of the landscape that makes the shot work; the wildlife just provides a sense of scale. I used to think that I could only shoot images on a sunny day, a limitation which, in Britain, turns us all into avid weather forecasters! Whilst it is true that there are some shots for which you need sunlight, these habitat shots generally need extreme light and/or weather conditions to show the habitat at its most impressive.

Habitats can mean different things to different people. For some, it is the urban environment that spurs them on and they simply cannot live or work outside it. As for me, well, I need wilderness, which is something that is

Opposite page:
Arctic tern and iceberg

becoming harder and harder to find. I am fortunate to have travelled to some of the world's most remote wildernesses and to have seen areas without any visible human footprints. Flying over the roof of South Georgia in a Royal Navy helicopter, door open and dressed snugly against the biting cold of this Southern Ocean oasis, I remember thinking that, apart from the odd derelict whaling station, there was no evidence of any human habitation at all. There were no footprints in the snow. Nothing. Here, all is pure and nature is firmly in control, wild and free. Wilderness Alaska has a similar feeling. Few of the remote and craggy mountains that rise up from the sea along the wild Katmai coast have ever been climbed and they probably never will be. It is the domain of the grizzly, the wolf and the fox, where bald eagles soar and salmon fight their way upstream for their final appointment with death. There are no tracks, no roads and no man-made colours. All is natural and pure. There is that word again. There is nothing more pure than nature itself in all her glory. It is this purity which I aim to capture in my habitat photography, simply because I am so inspired by it and want to show pure, unspoilt habitats free from any obvious effects of human intervention.

This type of photography is not something that can be learnt; it must be born out of a desire to be in the landscape. Colin Prior, who is a good friend of mine and one of the best landscape photographers on the planet, told me once that, in order to photograph the landscape, he had to sleep in it so that he felt part of it. He is so right. I am at my most creative when I am truly alone. This does not mean that I am some kind of recluse who cannot bear to be around other people –far from it. I just work best when I can escape the pressures of everyday life, however briefly... Once this happens I really begin to tune into the environment and start to feel a sense of actually belonging in it. Only then do I begin to see opportunities. That is when I produce my best habitat photography, as I am at my happiest and have no time pressures. Rather than taking snapshots, I have time to actually sit and wait for the light to come. I have curled up and fallen asleep countless times within penguin colonies or inside a tent in a remote Finnish forest listening to the screaming silence.

Sleeping in the wilderness allows me to make the transition between our modern, noisy civilization and the natural world. I fall asleep in a world full of pressure and expectation, and wake up in the wilderness with fresh energy and a clean slate, free to do what I like. In this world nobody judges me for anything I do; it is a wonderful feeling to have and it's a shame that all worlds are not like this one.

My only goal in publishing this portfolio is to help you better appreciate what we have in the world around us. Nature does not care if you are rich or poor,

Grizzly on alert

So many grizzly images fall into the same old cliché of a grizzly catching salmon. From my point of view, it seems a crime that the stunning habitat in which the grizzly lives is so often ignored. This female, who we called Nemo because of her fishing habits, was apprehensive about approaching the river as Ted, the dominant male, was already there. She stood up to get a better view and I straight away saw the habitat shot against the mountains behind.

Following pages (28-29):
Polar bear on blue ice

what car you drive or whether you are fat or thin. All it asks for is our respect and to be left alone. It is my personal view that we need to protect the habitat first and foremost and that is the underlying message of this portfolio. If we can protect areas and leave them untouched, then the ecosystems within them will have the best chance of survival. Mother Nature has managed perfectly well without our intervention for millions of years and she will do so long after we have conspired to remove ourselves from this planet. Mother Nature is the great survivor. All we have to do is to leave her alone to get on with it.

Sally lightfoot crab and morning wave

Crabs are great fun to work with as they tend to inhabit some interesting places and are active when the light is generally at its best. This sally lightfoot crab was feeding on the beach when I found it one early morning on Ascension Island. I liked the orange tint to the water and, to create something a little different, I let the waves have some motion to generate a softer feel to the image.

Walrus sleeping | Crabeater seals on iceberg

Here are two species of marine mammal that live on ice habitats at opposite ends of the earth. The left-hand image shows a group of walrus fast asleep against the backdrop of arctic Svalbard. The right-hand image shows a group of crabeater seals floating on an iceberg in Antarctica. In both cases, it is the awe-inspiring habitats that make these images so compelling and the sense of scale of the wildlife within them.

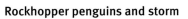

Rockhopper penguins and storm

Harsh weather makes for compelling wilderness images as it shows the brutal conditions in which animals survive. Here, four small colonies of rockhopper penguins are about to get battered by an approaching storm. The amazing penguins had no shelter. They just got on with life regardless and I did the same, hunching down on the hillside against the fierce winds and rain. Such weather is exhilarating for me and I love feeling the power of nature.

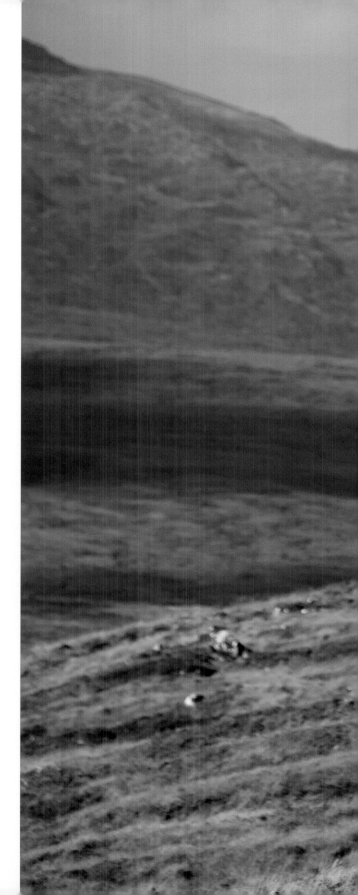

Red deer stag calling to hinds

Autumn in the Scottish Highlands is a wonderful time as the glens look glorious and there is a refreshing chill in the air. The haunting sounds of red deer stags in the middle of their annual rut echo throughout the mountains. It is an inspiring time for me to be out there, but also a real challenge as there is always a sniffing nose waiting to alert others to my presence. I move slowly, trying to blend with the landscape, dressed either as heather or bush and conscious that one mistake or one piece of bad luck would end my chances of an encounter that day. Most of the time I get nothing, but the possibility of getting an image like this one keeps me going. I was lucky with my position, being well concealed in a streambed with only my lens poking over the top. It had taken me hours of painstaking work to get close, but deer instinctively know when someone is around. Within a few minutes they had melted away into the hills, leaving me alone once again in the wilderness.

Common wildebeest and cloud formation | Bengal tiger on lake

Gentoo penguins on Mars

Penguins on Mars! Well it looks like it anyway, and that was my intention. The stark windswept plains of Sea Lion Island in the Falklands are home to several gentoo penguin colonies. This one is my favourite as it looks like the end of the earth. The day had been cloudy, but I know from experience that there is a chance of late sun as the weather is so changeable. Sure enough, I managed to get all of 20 seconds of light to record the penguins walking back home to the colony after a long day's hunting at sea. It's a bleak and desolate wilderness and not one in which you would normally expect to find penguins. They are such tough little characters.

Following pages (40-41):
Wildebeest herd and approaching storms

Grey seal at sunset | Sally lightfoot crab

*Two peaceful images that show how I have to actively look for these habitat shots
when the light is right. I had seen this grey seal earlier and thought that it would make
a lovely habitat shot at sunset. Once they are asleep, grey seals can be out for hours
so I knew that there was a good chance he would still be there and, as you can see, he
was. The sally lightfoot crab was filter feeding from rocks and clung on for dear life as
the waves crashed over it. I took a trick from professional landscape photographers by
giving the waves some motion to allow them to flow through the image and create an
impression of movement. I had to take the image before sunrise, as any light cast by
the sun over the water would have introduced an unwelcome distraction to the image
and removed the soft feel.*

Knot roost

Flocks of birds are a great ingredient for a habitat shot as they naturally form patterns within the landscape. This is a winter knot roost and has several thousand of the little waders within it. Most of the time the knot are sleeping and all is quiet, but once they decide to move off and feed, they do so en masse as a single living, breathing unit. This feeding motion can be found in the 'Patterns' portfolio later in this book, but for a habitat shot I decided to take a much simpler approach. The picture works because of the combination of the pattern of the knot roost, the dramatic morning clouds and the patterns left by the receding tide. It is a Living Landscape in every sense of the word.

Green turtle hatchling | Grizzly on Katmai coast

This young green turtle hatched almost at sunset and I followed its mad dash down to the water where it would begin life at sea. It is said that only 1 in 10,000 survive to reach maturity; let us hope that maybe this was the one. The grizzly image is one of many layers. It has the behavioural element of the grizzly in its never-ending search for food, combined with the wilderness element of the Katmai coast and Kodiak Island on the horizon. The gulls just happened to be in the right place at the right time. Living Landscapes such as these should be able to tell their own stories and they can only do so if the photographer feels what it is like to be in the landscape and has the passion to share it. It is easy for me as I just love grizzlies and always want to show them in the most positive fashion that I can.

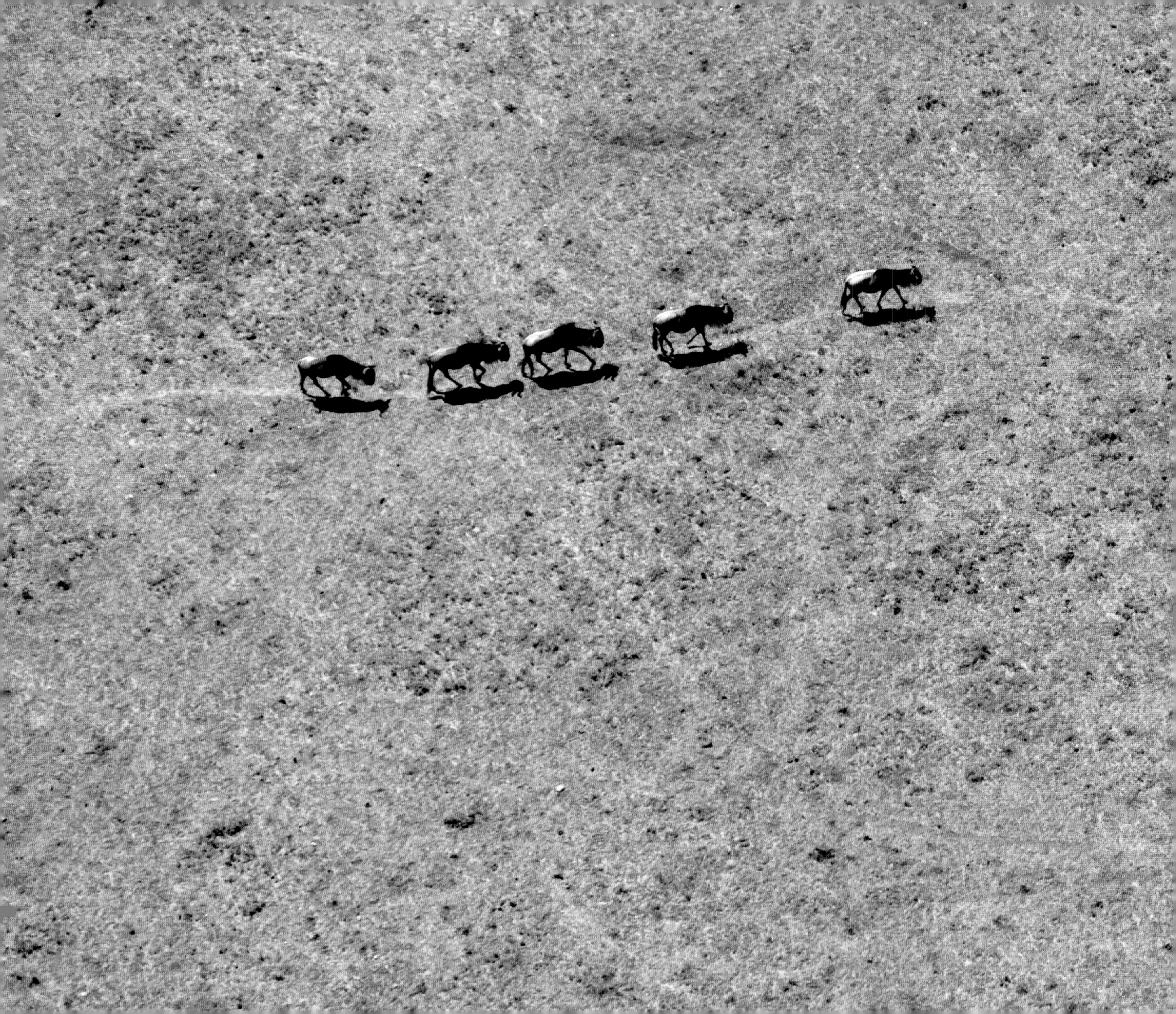

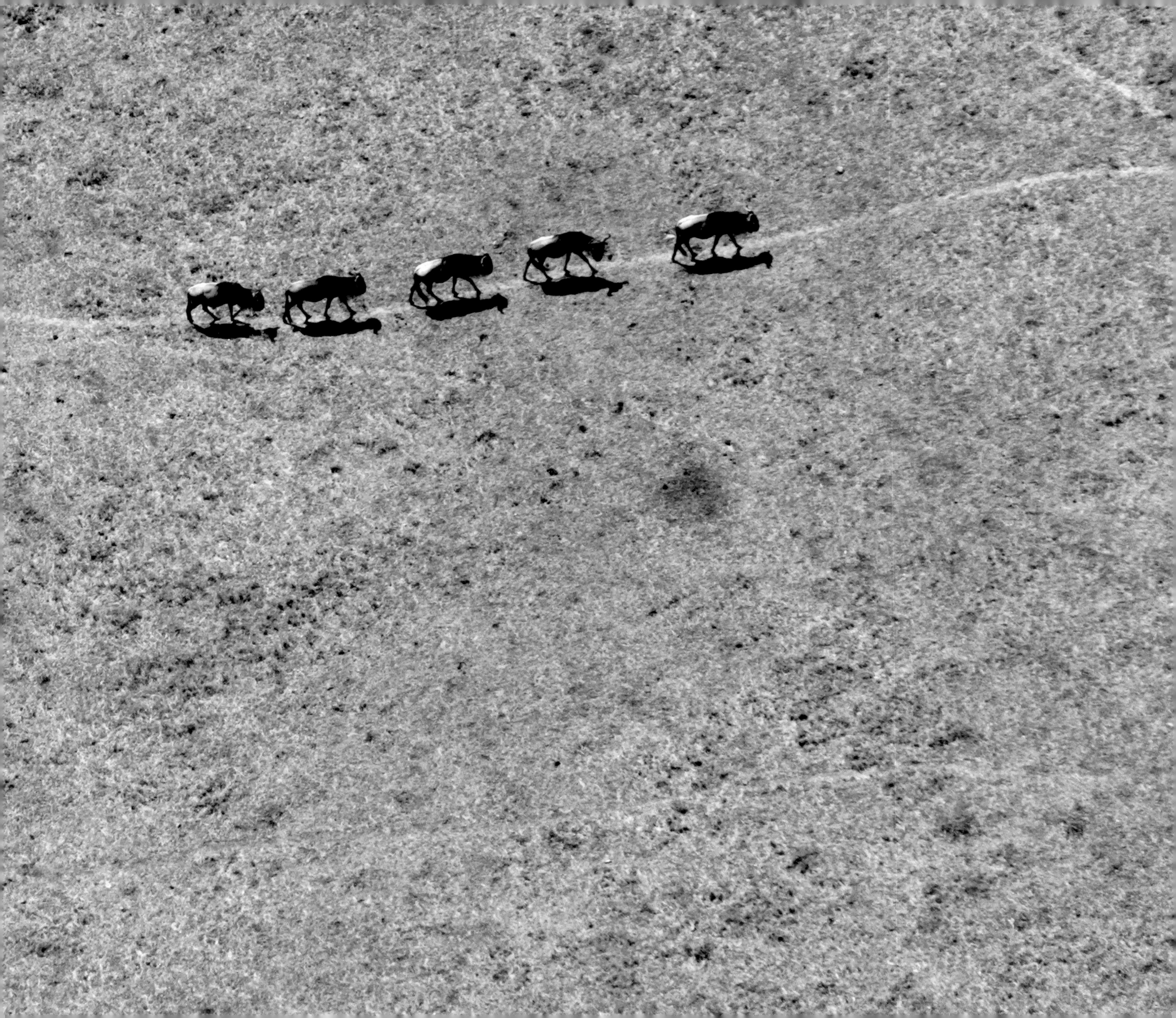

Mountain hare running | Polar bear in snowstorm
Ice is a wonderful subject to work with and always makes habitat images look that extra bit special. The mountain hare works because of the strong contrast between the intense blue sky and the stark, snow-covered mountainside, which really gives a feeling of the wilderness. It also was my only reward for eight hours struggling through waist deep snow. The polar bear is a little bit closer in the frame than most of the images in this portfolio, but it is allowed in this case, as the story here is of the snowstorm and the power of the habitat.

Previous pages:
Wildebeest walking on tracks

Wildebeest herd in rain

The first migration crossing I ever saw was amazing, so was the second and third. In fact, my 106th crossing, which is what you see here, was still amazing to Andy Rouse the naturalist. However, the photographer in me, having recorded thousands of images of wildebeest crossing rivers, was looking for something else. The light on this day was awful so I was tempted just to watch. Then the heavens opened and a sudden shower changed the setting completely. The rain added some extra drama and passion to create a shot that was not there before. The wildebeest probably did not notice the conditions – such is their desire to cross – but it suddenly became far more dangerous for them. The banks became as slippery as glass and as I watched, several plunged helplessly down the banks into the water. Stealthy predators like crocodiles are hard enough to see in perfect conditions, but when you are crossing a dark brown torrent with a surface splattered by rain, it is very much a case of crossing and hoping that it is your lucky day. Images like this that use weather conditions have just that little bit extra which lifts them above the standard record shot. It also makes you really respect these wildebeest; they are truly incredible animals.

Previous pages:
Barnacle geese formations

European brown bear in forest | Mountain gorillas relaxing

Namaqua chameleon in desert

Deserts must be one of the toughest habitats in which to survive and they are difficult places to work as a photographer. One desert I have experienced is the Namib in Southern Africa and this remains one of my favourite images from that time. We had driven for miles across the incredibly unforgiving and sparse habitat, seeing little wildlife, when suddenly a namaqua chameleon appeared from nowhere. We jumped out of the vehicle and the wall of heat hit us immediately. It was like a furnace and every breath was a struggle. The chameleon tolerated it with little or no shelter and it just carried on its business regardless. However, us sweaty humans needed to retreat to the vehicle after just a few minutes. I deliberately gave this image a lot of space, as I wanted to show the sparseness of the habitat and how incredibly tough a place this must be in which to survive for a day, let alone a lifetime.

Greater flamingos feeding
It was an incredible scene. The sun was rising over the mountain straight into my eyes, the morning mist was dancing across the water and hundreds of greater flamingos were busying themselves feeding. Sometimes words are just not enough...

Following pages (62-63):
Gentoo penguin stretching

SNOW GEESE

ANGELS IN THE SKY

By now you will realize that I find inspiration in all aspects of the natural world and not just the obvious wildlife that seems to win me awards. In fact, I find inspiration in the most unusual and unexpected places. I certainly did not anticipate that a simple trip to photograph snow geese in New Mexico at the invitation of the great bird photographer Artie Morris would set personal challenges that would inspire me almost to the point of obsession. Geese have always had a special place in my photographic heart and I have spent many cold mornings on the Scottish island of Islay waiting for the barnacle geese to fly across Loch Suinart to their feeding grounds. There is just something about geese that draws me to photograph them, but to be honest, I really can't say what that is. What I do know is that my time with snow geese changed my perception of my work and pushed me to levels of creativity that I would never have thought possible.

Snow geese undertake one of the most incredible migrations on the planet. From their breeding grounds in Arctic Canada, they fly along defined routes called flyways to their feeding grounds many thousands of miles to the south. The flight of the snow geese was immortalized in a stunning piece of cinematography by Des and Jen Bartlett and it has fascinated generations. The exploits of the snow geese are followed each year by millions on the worldwide web but currently there is concern about them, as their flyways are changing. Whether this is due to some man-made effects or is just a natural phenomenon is yet to be seen. I had read about all these things, but understood them only as a dry compilation of facts. Now I wanted to see the reality and experience the emotion for myself. So it was at the world-famous Bosque del Apache reserve in New Mexico that I started my quest.

I remember my first morning like it was yesterday. Artie had shown me on the map where to go and when I arrived the car park was full and there was a buzz in the air. The atmosphere felt akin to a football match at the end of the season, which is very different to the usual sombre and intense mood experienced at most wildlife gatherings. Photographers were fiddling with their tripods and I was pleased to see families with excited small children getting dressed up against the cold. It is always great to see future generations being shown what they will inherit and taught what they must

Opposite page:
Snow geese blast-off

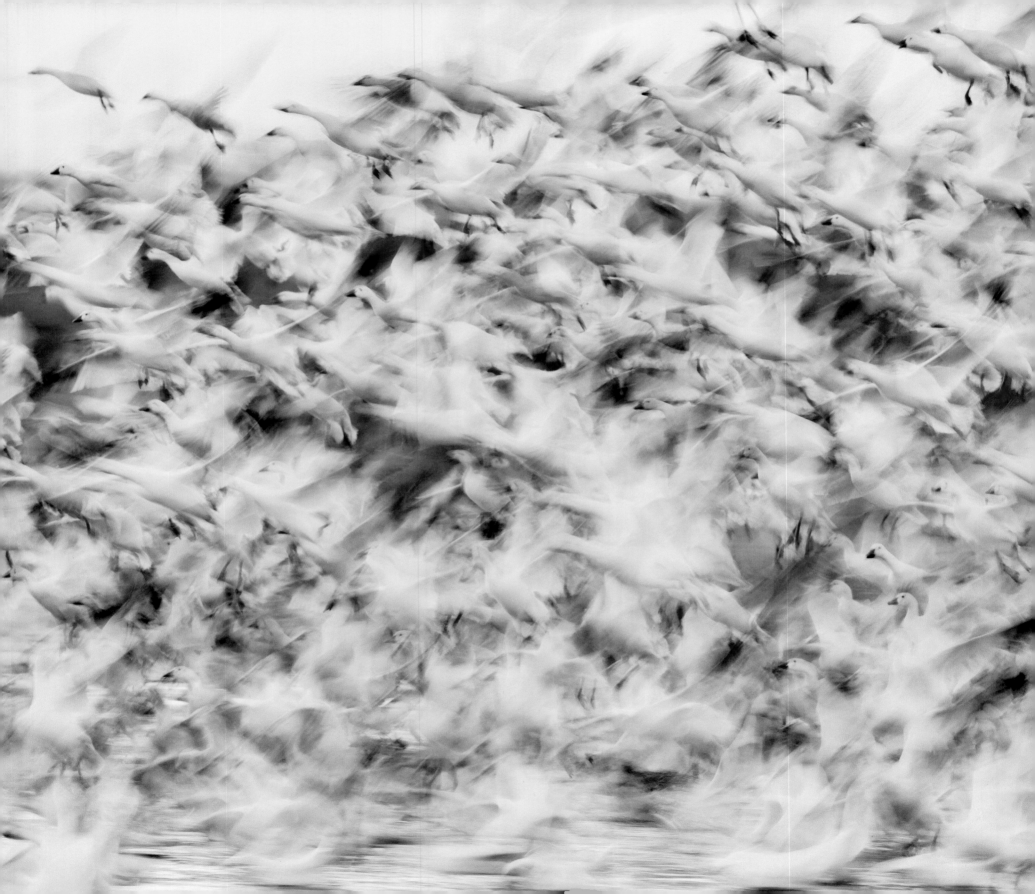

Snow geese festival

The snow geese put on an incredible show and, whenever they fly overhead, I am just compelled to watch and I am not alone. The annual festival that coincides with the arrival of the geese at Bosque del Apache packs the reserve for several days with fellow addicts. To see kids smiling in wonder and waving as the geese fly by brings real warmth to my heart. Perhaps there is hope for the future of our wildlife after all.

protect. Slowly, I made my way along a narrow track into the frigid darkness where mountains loomed in front of me, casting a sinister silhouette against the night sky. Somewhere close at hand, I knew, there were several thousand snow geese, bright, shining white geese, but in the darkness, all was just black. Then I caught a faint sound on the wind; somewhere out there in the night a snow goose had called. Quietly, I sat down in the long grass, arranged my paraphernalia around me and waited expectantly for something to happen. I didn't have a clue what that was, but these times for me are always the most exhilarating.

After a few minutes, my eyes adjusted to the light and gradually I began to see white shapes in the distance. As dawn approached, I quickly realized that there were a lot of geese right in front of me and I mean a LOT of geese. Then, right at the limits of my hearing, I began to hear the sound of geese calling; straining my eyes in the general direction of the sound, I saw thousands flying towards me silhouetted against the first light of dawn. They continued calling until they were directly overhead and then, with a final squawk, peeled off and landed amongst the mass in front of me. The noise levels rose as enthusiastic greetings were exchanged. As the minutes ticked by, more and more geese approached and landed, until the lake was completely covered by white shapes milling around. They didn't seem to be doing much apart from chattering to each other and I wondered if that was it for the day as geese are eating machines once their brief morning flight is over. I settled in for a long wait in the hope that one might come close – little did I know what was about to happen.

Thirty seconds later I found out. As the first rays of the morning sun burst over the horizon, the geese went deathly quiet and all around was silence. Then, without a sound, the first goose erupted from the back of the lake, struggling to get into the cold morning air. Like a rolling wave, the rest of the flock began to take off, turning the silence into an incredible crescendo of noise as thousands of wing beats made their own natural symphony. Within seconds over half the flock were in the air calling excitedly to each other like nothing I have ever heard. The noise was incredible and nothing can describe it in words; you just had to be there to hear it. I just sat open-mouthed as the wave of noise rolled my way and the lead goose flew thirty feet above my head. The lake emptied as finally they were all in the air, the leaders already starting to head east to their favourite farmland feeding grounds. Their calls died away and were replaced by the excited chattering all around me. I looked around at my human companions and everyone was smiling. During the peak of the blast-off, the kiddies next to me had jumped up and down cheering. This was the amazing effect that such a fantastic natural spectacle had. Their mood was infectious and I found I was grinning too. It was a high that was to become an addiction. Each day after the blast-off, I would feel elation which would then be replaced by a thirst for more and I couldn't wait for the next morning. I was hooked immediately.

As the days wore on, the nature lover in me was on sensory overload but the photographer (and some would say my darker side) was getting more and more dissatisfied with the pictures I was taking of the geese. My Living Landscape efforts, showing nice shots of geese in the beautiful New Mexico habitat, were pretty cool, but they were the exception. Everything else was technically perfect, well composed and exposed – but utterly emotionless. Clearly I had some thinking to do, as my pictures so far had captured little of what I actually felt. Being able to express my feelings is the main driving force behind my photography these days.

One lunchtime, I went to one of those typical mom and pop Mexican diners that can be found right across New Mexico. As I sat munching my food, a small gaggle of geese flew over me, shining pure white against the intensely blue desert sky. I am not sure if it was the fire in my stomach from the chillies or the proverbial lightning bolt, but at that moment I began to see the geese with very different eyes. They reminded me of something, but try as I might, I couldn't think what it was. It bugged me for some time but eventually I realized what it was. With the pure white of their feathers against the blue sky, they conjured up in my imagination a vision of a flock of angels flying overhead. Fanciful perhaps, but if you believe in angels, then you would be hard pressed to find anything else in the natural world that fits the bill so readily. My creative side finally started to wake up.

The change in my photography was instant. Gone were the record shots and in their place was art; the emotion was there for all to see. I began to work with the early spectacular morning blast-offs and immediately stopped recording them as freeze-frame 'puppet' images (I call them that because they look like a load of snow geese puppets on a string) but as a living, moving entity. When I watched a blast-off, I didn't see it frozen in time but as a constantly changing and evolving shape in front of me; a wave that gathered momentum. That is what I wanted to show; a blur of life. So I started to experiment by taking long exposures to create a greater sense of motion and elegance. I also started to wonder what it must be like to be one of the geese right in the centre of the blast-off, where the cacophony of noise and beating wings would be at its peak. It must offer an incredible feeling of belonging and a sense of exhilaration to be right in the thick of the action. Using a long lens, something that is becoming more of a stranger to me these days, I focused on a few geese right in the centre of the action and followed them as they took off through the mass. I was just in the mood to try anything and felt so alive and inspired.

Snow geese
It always pays not to rush and to take time to get the best angle. I chose this position to get a combination of the intense colour on the lake and the geese on their final approach to bring some balance to the top corners.

I think my most interesting work from this period came when I was trying to illustrate the angel concept a little more clearly. Geese are creatures of habit and I worked out a place where they regularly flew overhead against the stunning blue New Mexico sky. I watched several groups flying over and they were all in uniform formations. In my limited experience of such matters this was not how I envisaged angels might fly. I imagined an angel to be ethereal, a mysterious being which probably didn't squawk at its neighbour like a snow goose! I realized that I had to adapt what I was literally seeing in order for it to become my vision of an angel. The only way I could do that was to create motion trails in the sky behind them, to transition the images into art. Anyone watching me achieve this would have concluded that I was practising semaphore or engaging in some weird tribal dance involving the worship of a camera! I just let my creativity flow and soon the angels began to take shape in real life...

The images you see here are experimental, beyond doubt, but I feel they are some of my most creative and visionary pieces of work to date. I wanted to include them to show that, with photography, there are no boundaries to your self-expression; creativity must always come first. So if you have an idea, nurture it and let it blossom into reality as it may make all your dreams come true. Always remember that provided you are happy with the results no-one has the right to tell you otherwise. Photography is an art form where self-expression rules and beauty is definitely in the eye of the beholder.

Snow geese mountain sunrise
This is nature in all its glory. The pre-dawn glow cast a red hue across the desert landscape and I could have cut the silence with a knife. The geese...well they just looked part of the landscape, which they are.

Following pages (70-71):
Afternoon clouds over feeding snow geese

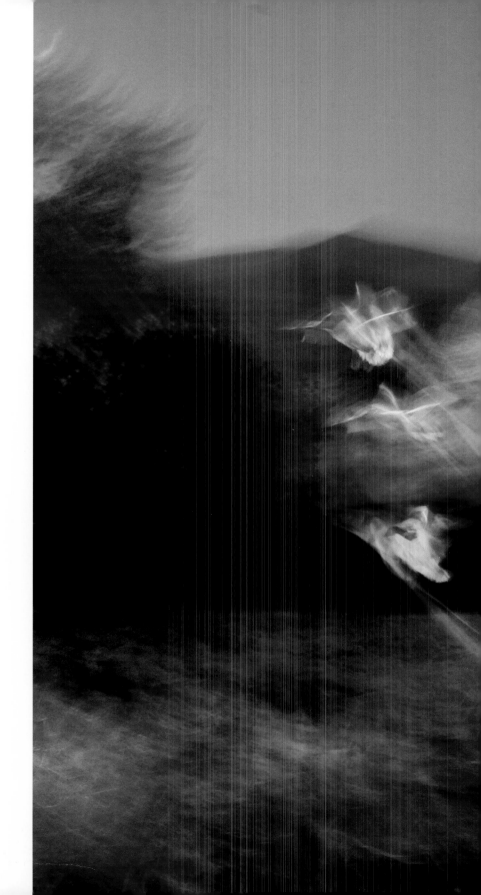

Snow geese landing

My creative images are usually planned and triggered by some subconscious desire to be different. I had already photographed geese coming in to land at this spot several times before, as I loved the autumn colours of the cottonwoods behind. It was a beautiful evening, all was silent around me and, for once, I was alone with the geese. First, I took some straight images to freeze the motion of the incoming geese; they looked great with wings outstretched, fighting the effects of gravity. They were damn nice shots too, but as usual this wasn't enough for me. As I already had some cool shots in the camera, I decided to experiment and look at the landings from a different viewpoint. So along came creative me, and here are the results. I liken this to being a rock singer where for most of your recording life, you write rock songs that are the norm for the genre and you are known for it. However, occasionally you may want to do something different and break out of that mould, so you write a ballad instead. Of course, some people hate it, but in the end everyone accepts that it is just the 'same old you' expressing yourself in another way. As a professional photographer these days you need to have more than one string in your bow...

Snow geese patterns | Snow geese aerial

Two vastly different interpretations of flight are shown here. The very artistic one above shows the beautiful lines of the geese in flight with a creative twist from yours truly. You may not recognize them as geese, but they certainly make stunning natural patterns that catch the eye. The right-hand image is an aerial and I love the long shadows of the flying geese against the lake.

Following pages (76-77):
Snow geese close up

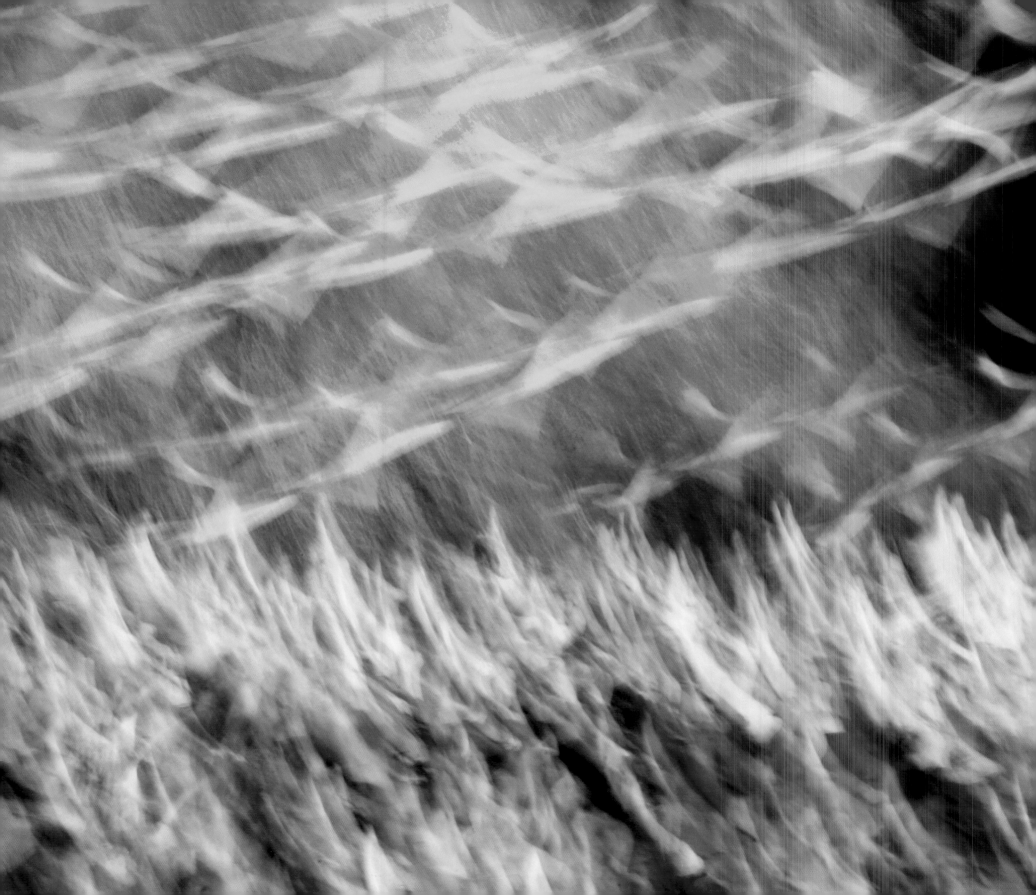

Snow geese and paper airplanes

*I know, paper airplanes! Somehow I have managed to create
paper airplanes from snow geese and it was completely by
accident. It was late in the afternoon and the geese had settled
all together on the one lake that was very difficult to photograph.
A few were milling round overhead trying to find a place to land
and after taking a few of the standard shots, I decided to slow
things down a little to see if I could get some streaky lines across
the top. Well I managed to get more than I bargained for and
once I saw this effect, I spent a lot of exposures getting it to the
paper airplanes that you see here.*

Previous pages:
Snow geese abstract

Following pages (82-83):
Snow geese taking off from lake

Following pages (84-85):
Snow geese rowing

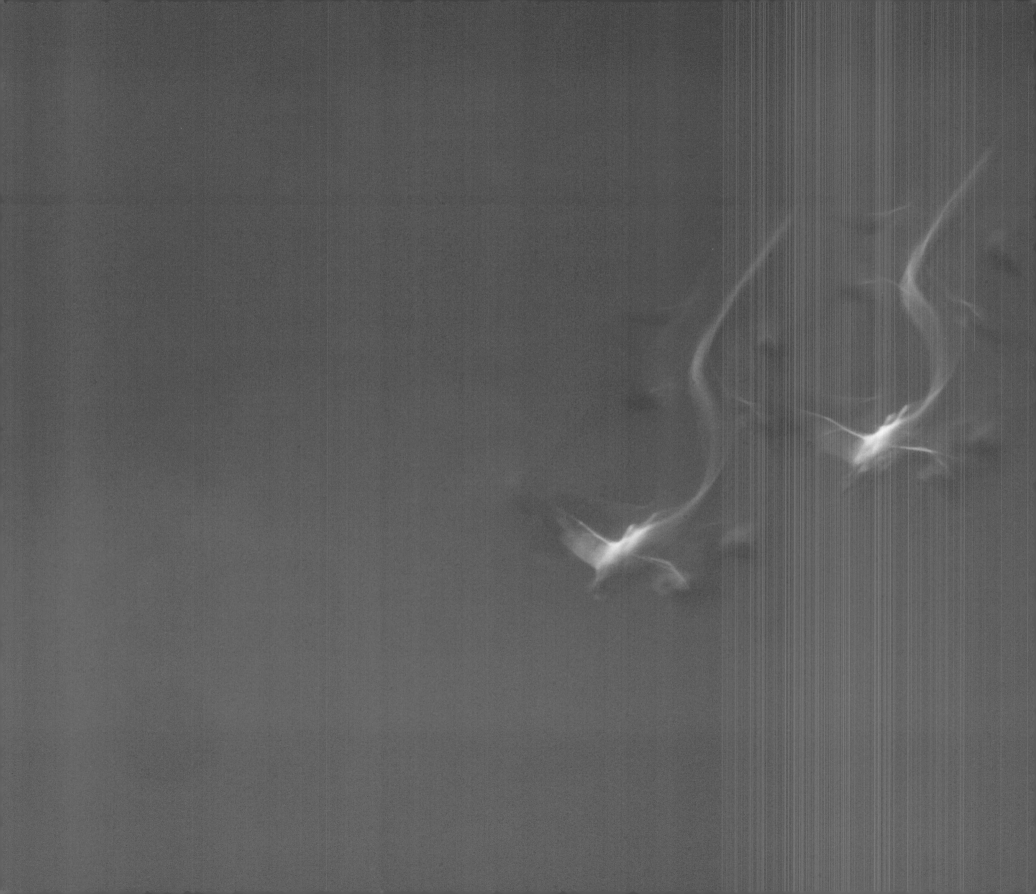

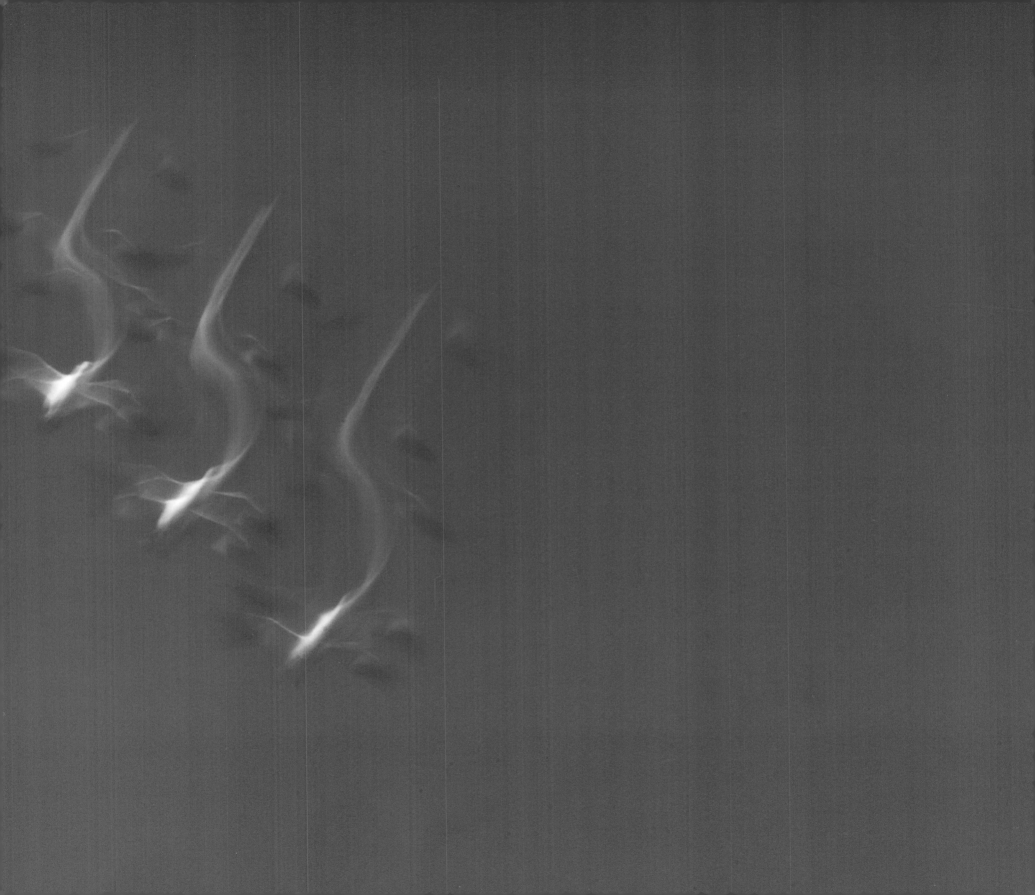

Snow geese landing | Snow geese at sunrise
*These are two very simple shots. I love the focused looks of the geese landing in the
left-hand image. They have decided where they are going to set down and nothing will
stop them. The wider-angle shot is a more traditional Living Landscape and combines
the elements of light, landscape and a recognizable subject into a nice image.*

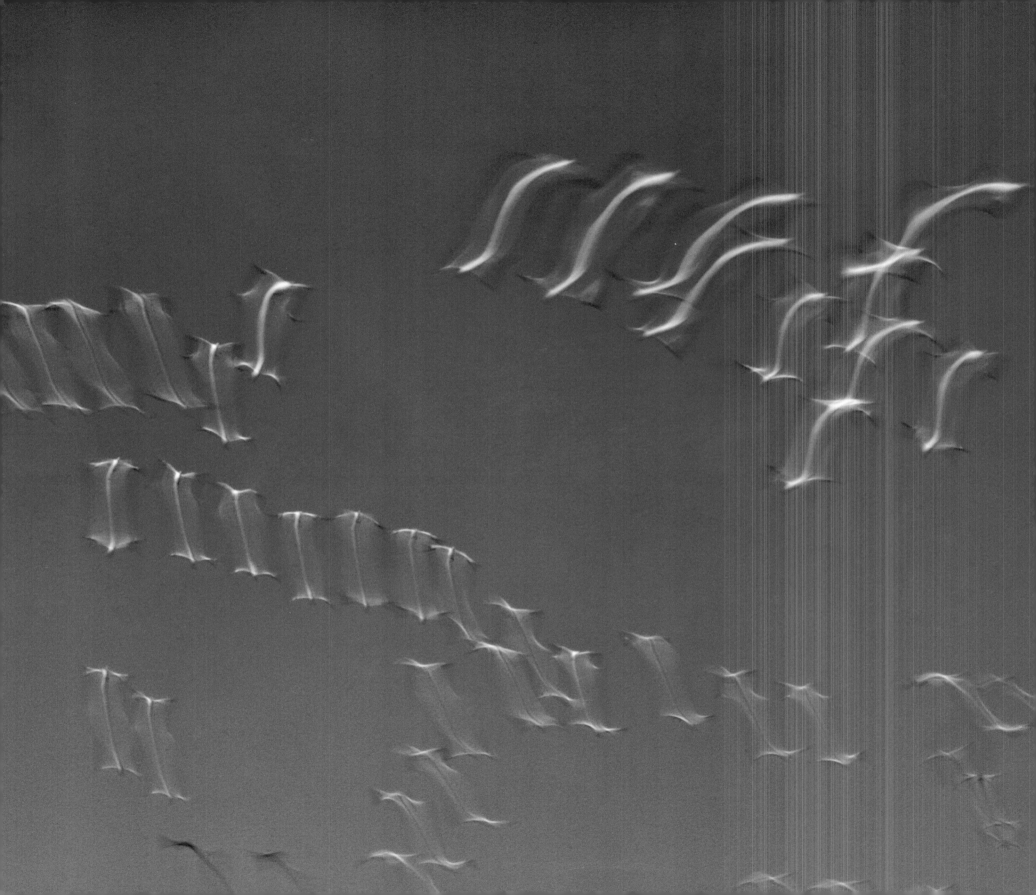

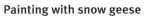

Painting with snow geese

I really love these experimental shots as they use the motion of the geese to produce natural patterns in the sky. In fact, rather than painting with light (a common technique for creative night-time landscape photography) I am actually painting with geese! I always see hieroglyphics when I look at this image and if you look carefully, you can actually see the individual wing beats. Of course, in this modern day and age, many will think that this image has been digitally altered to produce this effect. All I can say against this is that those of us with a creative eye and a desire to truthfully record what we see, will create our own shots in the camera.

Snow geese head-on | Snow geese at sunrise
*It is the chaos of the blast-offs that I really feel inspired to capture, but only once have
I managed to get one head-on. You can see here how tightly packed the geese are,
which is a complete contrast to the image above where they seem to have all the
space in the world.*

A rolling wave of snow geese
Blast-offs are simply incredible. Like a rolling wave, they start from the rear, gathering momentum, as more geese get airborne. The noise of the wings is something that I will never forget.

PATTERNS

SEEING IS BELIEVING

I hope you will realize that this book is intended to showcase elements of my photography that challenge the norm and to illustrate the beauty and complexity of the natural world from an alternative viewpoint. My images for magazines and newspapers are more orthodox because they have to be very simple and easy to understand. They are intended to capture someone's attention immediately, even if they are just idly flicking through it and not sure whether to buy the paper or not. It is a fact of life that the commercial photography market generally prefers straight shots, i.e. portraits with no background and animals that are pretty full in the frame. This makes sense as the clients have to choose the images that they feel will best convey their message to the reader. Because of this, I have to conform a bit in order to continue funding my passion for spending my life with animals. Unfortunately this does put my financial interests at odds with my creative self these days, because the images that really inspire me are those that people do not expect me to take. The images reproduced on the next few pages cannot be absorbed at a simple glance. However, if you pause to study them and allow them to ask questions of your imagination, I hope you will feel it is worth that extra time. These photographs which can only be fully absorbed after a second, or even a third, look are what I call 'double-take' images'.

Visual patterns are a familiar part of our everyday lives and the urge to discover them seems to be hard-wired into our brains. All photographers use patterns in their photography, even if they are unaware of it, and macro photographers have always looked for the amazing patterns of the inner world. The images that you see here are not macro images in the technical sense at all since most are taken with a long lens. Instead, these images take their inspiration from many sources, of which one of the most important is the work of the French photographer Yann Arthus-Bertrand. I first saw his work in his 'Earth from the Air' exhibition and I remember staring at each image for minutes on end, revelling in the patterns and textures that he had captured from the air. They were, and still are, just incredible and I have taken so much inspiration from studying how he interprets both natural and man-made patterns. I never have a problem in recognizing the fact that another photographer has inspired me to push my own boundaries and I freely acknowledge that some of the pictures in this book have been directly influenced by his work.

Opposite page:
Starling ball

Starlings over canal

A combination of wildlife and man-made objects can be a really nice mix and can illustrate a sense of scale. Without the canal boats and tree, you would have little idea how big the starlings actually are. It also puts them in context, as they are predominantly an urban species.

I dabbled with a Bertrand-like style for years with some very ropey attempts, but it was during my time in South Georgia working with the Royal Navy that I really began to see the images emerging. The scale of the wildlife to be found within the jaw-dropping scenery of South Georgia is incredible and I remember one day in particular when I saw a pattern that influenced so much of what I do today. I was in a Royal Navy helicopter, hovering just off-shore from St Andrews Bay, and as I looked out of the door I could see, 2000 feet below me, one of the largest king penguin colonies in the world. From this height, I could not distinguish individuals but could only see the contrasting patterns of the brown youngsters grouped together in crèches amongst the white adults. Within those patterns, I could see snakes, outlines of familiar countries and a host of other shapes that fired my imagination. When you look at this image in the portfolio, it is the sense of scale, or rather the lack of it, that causes the double take. This is a good trick for creating these images. If you remove all sense of scale, then the viewer will be more likely to take a longer look at your image to try to work out what it shows.

Mother Nature has an endless pattern book and you do not necessarily have to be 2000 feet up in the air in order to see examples of it. For example, chameleon skin is beautiful in its simplicity, land iguana skin can look like sweetcorn and the veins in an elephant's ear can look like a map of a lost world. Nature's patterns are out there right now, waiting to be photographed; it is just up to you to see them. I certainly do not spot them in every case, especially if I am pushed for time and needing to shoot quickly, or if I am simply not in the right frame of mind to create these kind of images. Indeed, adequate time was the main factor in determining the quality of the images in this portfolio, as time was needed to visualize and plan them. They simply could not be rushed. Usually such images are made when I am able to sit down, relax and absorb my surroundings. This is when the patterns start to show themselves and I can set about capturing them for others to enjoy. I think that the one thing I have learned from this kind of photography is the importance of not rushing any of my photography, or indeed, these days, my life. Hopefully the results will convince you to do the same. After all, it is much better to get one good image than a card full of near misses.

Use of scale is one way to create a double-take image, but sometimes it is the beauty and subtlety of motion that can tell a wonderful story and create intrigue. By motion, I do not mean the two-dimensional type of motion image that is frozen in time – although there is a place for that in my photography, just not in this portfolio. Instead the aim here is to make an image that flows across the page and into the imagination. If successful, such pictures occupy a no-man's land, somewhere between stills photography and moving images. They show motion as a constantly changing and evolving shape that triggers emotions. In several portfolios in this book, you will see images of this kind. My favourites are the slow-motion blast-off sequences in the Snow Geese portfolio. I have one of these images blown up as a canvas hanging on my wall and every day I see something different in it. I get something new out of this picture every time because it is multi-dimensional and screams for attention. On my walls I have several of my favourite images taken over the course of my career, but it is always this image that my visitors are drawn to, and most spend several minutes looking at it, then looking at it once again. This is what I am trying to achieve with this portfolio. I want you to look at all the images here and let them trigger your own imagination. From imagination comes creativity and becoming more creative will only benefit your own photography. Personally, it would mean so much to me if someone reading this won an award and said, 'Andy Rouse inspired me to try this' – it really would.

Marine iguana landscape
Patterns do not always have to be uniform to work. In fact they can be chaotic and still be interesting! This image combines the elements of a wild Living Landscape with an interesting foreground pattern of hissing, spitting marine iguanas!

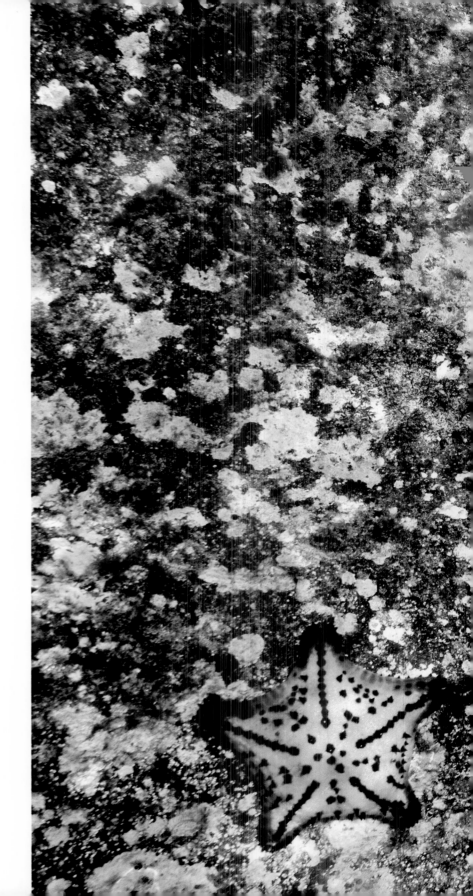

Galapagos green turtle and sea stars

A lot of my pictures rely on beautiful animals to make them work and to generate the main interest. This Galapagos green turtle is certainly beautiful, but it is not the main element of this Living Landscape. It has to vie for attention with the rocks, the algae on which it feeds, the stunning sea stars and the fish that are omnipresent whenever a turtle is feeding. Its shell may be beautiful and the intricate symmetry of the sea star appealing, but they are not immediately apparent and it takes time to fully appreciate their details. This time element is the essence of any Living Landscape as it takes more than a quick glance to unravel and reveal the secrets of these images. The turtle couldn't have cared less about my Living Landscape or me – it was happily asleep!

Previous pages:
Land iguana eye

Following pages (102-103):
King penguin colony from the air

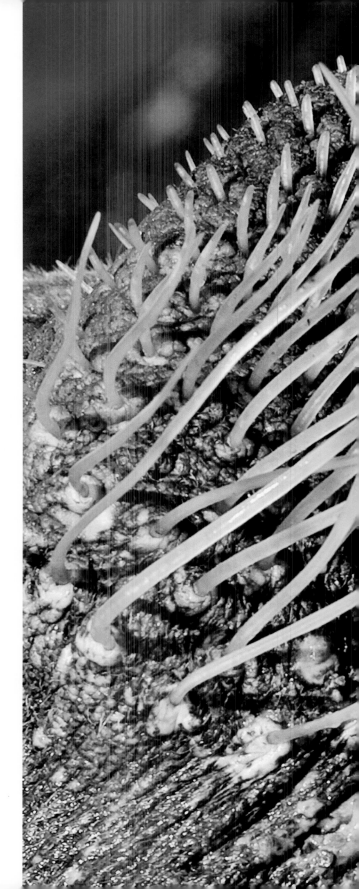

Walrus whiskers
Weird, huh? At first glance, you might think that you are looking at the plastic bristles on a hairbrush, but you would be wrong! These are in fact the facial whiskers of an Atlantic walrus, one of the sea elephants of the Arctic Ocean. The whiskers are used to feel for food on the dark floor of the ocean as they primarily feed on small invertebrates. Also, did you know that a male walrus can weigh up to two tons? That's several times more than the largest male polar bear.

Previous pages:
Wildebeest herd in motion

Following pages (108-109):
African elephant abstract

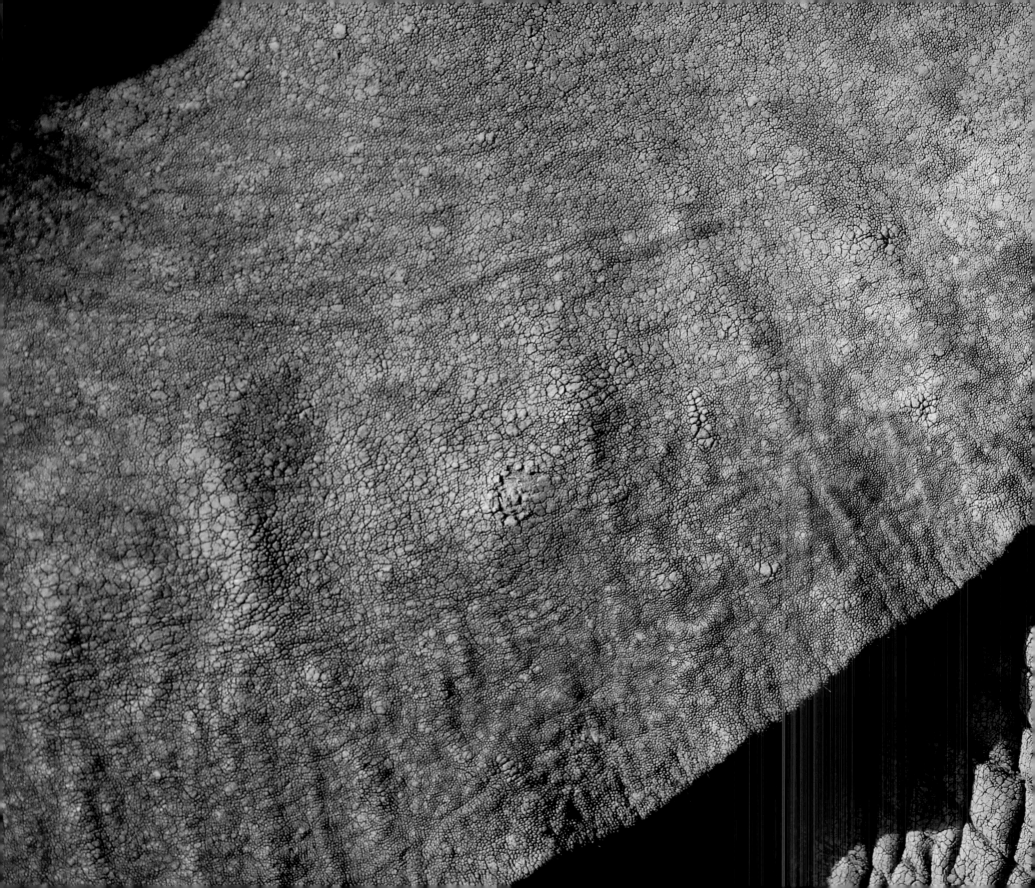

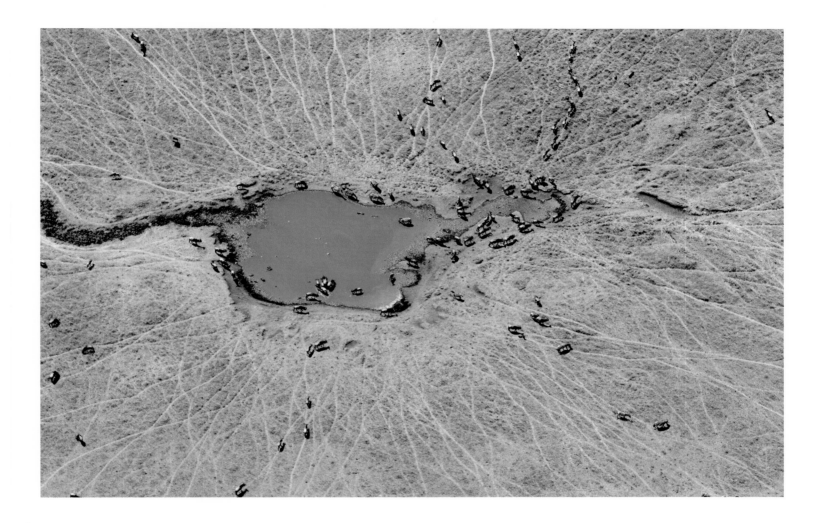

Stonefish camouflage | Wildebeest at waterhole

Both images are looking straight down from above and both have an absence of any scale. As I have said previously, this is quite deliberate. The left-hand shot shows a stonefish that I saw whilst snorkeling in the Galapagos. It is an incredible colour and blends perfectly with the reef, but camouflage isn't its only defence – those barbs are very poisonous to anything that tries to eat it or tread on it. Check out the amazing eyes on top. The picture above shows a waterhole being frequented by wildebeest during their migration. When I first flew over this, I was drawn to the patterns of the tracks as they converged on the water.

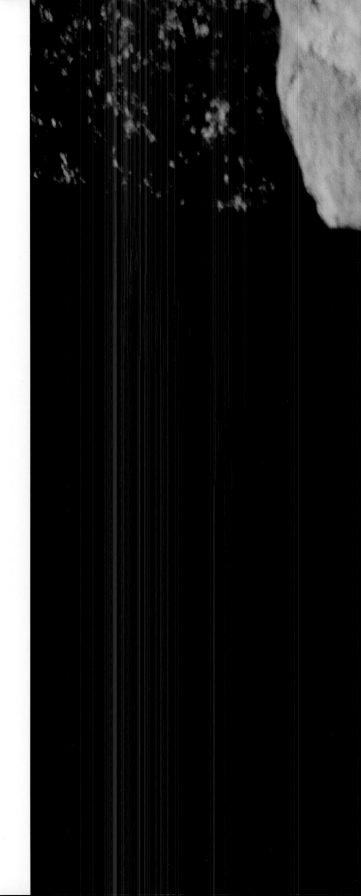

Leopard shadow

Leopards are stunning cats and it is so difficult to resist anything other than a lovely shot of the head. This is great as a starting point, but once you have it (and believe me, it can take a lifetime of trying) it is time to try something different. This shot here is certainly something different, as it doesn't actually show the leopard at all, just its shadow against the rock. What it does do is to capture the essence of a leopard – which is a stealthy hunter, a ghost in the grass. Cats like lions are easy to find, as all you have to do is to look for the nearest shady tree under which you will find one snoring its head off. However, leopards only show themselves when they want to, so any picture of them needs to reflect this trait. I think that this shadow shot really captures the shy nature of this incredibly elusive cat.

Wildebeest shadows

Perhaps the easiest form of aerial photography is from a hot air balloon. It is a wonderful experience to drift sedately across the plains on a beautiful clear morning. Provided the pilot holds the balloon above 100ft, the wildebeest don't seem to mind too much either. Although I saw the potential of this image almost straight away, it took me a while to isolate a small group of wildebeest that would keep the image simple. I wanted to shoot the image from directly overhead as the shadows needed to be the main story and I wanted the bodies of the wildebeest to blend into the grassland. Since I could not turn the balloon around for a second go, it was effectively a one-shot deal which is proof that creativity and timing wins over technology every time.

Land iguana skin | Knot flock flying

These two patterns may look different but they are both made of small, interrelated elements. The shot above is the well-worn skin of a male land iguana; he has had many battles and has the scars to prove it. The right-hand image shows a flock of knot flying after being attacked by a peregrine falcon. Knot are amazing waders to watch as they wheel in the sky, moving as one.

Knot flock

On this particular morning we found the knot flock close to the shore and seemingly very relaxed. Most of them were asleep with their heads tucked under their wings. The pattern was lovely and for a while it was a very peaceful scene. There are always a few alert eyes, though, as trouble is never far away, and sure enough, a few worried calls woke everyone up as keen eyes had seen a falcon somewhere. The knot began to get more agitated and really move around. This gave me an idea, so I found a knot that was static and used it as the focus for the shot. By using a long exposure I managed to blur the moving birds and in doing so created a real feeling of the flock in motion.

PLANET GALAPAGOS

WHERE NORTH MEETS SOUTH

There are some places that you just have to see before you die and, for me, Galapagos is right up there with the Pyramids and the Taj Mahal. Forever associated with the name of Charles Darwin and a long-time favourite of TV documentary makers, this group of nineteen volcanic islands and 105 islets has become synonymous with conservation. Darwin spent a great deal of time on the Galapagos during his six-year cruise on HMS *Beagle* and it was there that he gathered much of the evidence on which he would later base his theory of evolution through natural selection. Now it is the undisputed number one destination for eco-tourists as its diversity of wildlife, and the fact that the creatures appear to have no fear of humans at all, make it a very special place to visit.

For years I had put off visiting the Galapagos because of the eco-tourism. I knew what I wanted the Galapagos to be and I did not want to be disappointed. Fortunately, the archipelago is amazingly well controlled and protected by the Galapagos National Park Authority and it fully lived up to all my expectations. As a photographer, though, I am glad that I waited until I was good enough to appreciate what I saw and do it justice. As with all equatorial islands, the light is challenging at the best of times, the wildlife can be difficult for all their friendliness and the story is more about the environment than the species that live within it. However, it is a true Living Landscape and that is why it was important for me to include it in this book.

You probably think I am mad to say that friendly wildlife is more difficult to photograph than subjects which are nervous or elusive. Well, the fact is that when animals are so cooperative it is easy to become complacent and take the easy option, forgetting about creativity. So whilst it is extremely simple to get lots of pictures on the Galapagos, getting great pictures is another matter entirely. My strategy is always to sit and watch what is happening, work out what message I want the picture to convey and then how I am going to use the light to depict this. Sometimes it works and sometimes it doesn't, but whilst the Galapagos did sometimes frustrate Rouse the photographer, they never disappointed Rouse the animal-lover.

Opposite page:
Land iguana close-up

One day on Genovesa Island, I was sitting with two friends, David and Shaun, watching two masked boobies that were engrossed in their courtship and

Marine iguana with friendly lava lizard
Photographing nature is a serious business, but there is always an element of humour too. I saw this image of a lava lizard on top of a marine iguana and really loved the scale of it and the fun element.

Following pages (124-125):
Red cardinal shoal

nest-building rituals. It was mid-afternoon, the sun was high and it was blistering hot; it was impossible to do anything but, hey, it was sunny and warm. So we sat for two hours waiting for the light to get better, and all the time I was observing the boobies and planning what I wanted to do with the pair of them. The sun sank slowly towards the horizon and, finally, I began to see some detail in their white chest feathers and knew that soon it would be time to take my first shots. However, I still had a problem. The light was stunning, the birds were beautiful, but there was an element missing – the landscape. The area that the boobies had chosen to nest in was filled with distractions and I did not just want a shot of the birds for the sake of it. So I had think again and quickly realized that I needed to change the landscape in the shot by changing the angle from which I photographed it. Lying down onto my stomach, I saw that the out-of-focus foreground and background created by the low angle made a natural frame around the courting couple. It was a lovely shot with an ethereal feel. As I watched the male went walkabout only to return with a twig that he proudly presented to the female to place on their nest. Twig-passing complete, they raised their beaks and touched the ends; everything came together for a beautiful few seconds and the hours of waiting were worthwhile. I had my shot, she had her twig and it was beer o'clock.

Of course, the essence of any Living Landscape image is to try to show the relationships within it. The species that I had the most creative fun with (in fact, fun full stop) were the marine iguanas because they always seemed to be in the right place at the right time! I took great pleasure in including distant volcanoes or lava flows in my shots, with the sleeping, hissing or spitting iguanas in the foreground. Sometimes I took the close-up option, as their faces were incredibly prehistoric, full of character and really suited to one of my 'Just Plain Beautiful' portraits, as featured in *Concepts of Nature*. For me, they really personified the essence of the Galapagos – a world that has survived untouched through time.

The Galapagos is amazing above the waves, but it is truly incredible underneath them. I snorkelled for at least an hour on most days and had the most fantastic encounters with sea lions, marine iguanas and turtles. However, it was the turtles that really won my heart during my underwater experiences, as they always looked so helpless to me in the water, despite their agility and speed.

One encounter that will stay with me forever occurred when I was lucky enough to swim with a female green turtle for over an hour. We were in a small cove and there wasn't much shallow water for me to play with. In fact, the drop off to the deep was extreme, but along the sides of the rock walls were patches of coral, algae and sea grass that provided an easy food source for the turtle. The current was pretty rough and I was tossed against the rocks a few times, but never once did she seem disturbed by my presence. At one point, she was actually swimming to the surface to catch a breath when she must have noticed her own reflection in the dome port of my underwater housing. She came right over immediately and looked into it and then straight into my eyes. We just hung there – man and turtle – and for a few seconds, there was something special between us. Then suddenly, with a single beat of her flippers, she was off, taking a quick breath and moving away to start feeding again. This time I left her alone and made my way back to the ship. For a while I felt very elated but then strangely empty. I had enjoyed this encounter so much and was so relaxed with her that I did not want it to end. Special encounters like this are very rare and their rarity is what makes wildlife photography addictive; encounters like this just stir the passion inside me.

There is no doubt that the Galapagos is an incredible place and to travel there is a real privilege. It may sound like a cliché, but it does feel like stepping back in time. However, it is a threatened wilderness. On land, animals such as feral goats, cats and cattle (introduced by humans) wreck the fragile habitats of native species and find them easy prey. The marine environment is threatened by the illegal fishing of some of its most protected species due to their perceived value to humans and also by the sheer number of tourist vessels that ply the waters. One fear that I have always had about any wilderness is the danger of pollution from the oil industry. Recently, the grounding of an oil tanker posed the threat of just such a disaster on the Galapagos and served as a reminder that it would take only one accident to ruin this Eden forever. The Galapagos is unique; let us all try to keep them that way.

Volcanic habitat

The remote island of Cerro Dragon is a really beautiful place and one where the landscape photographer in me really started to take over. The odds are always against me though as I always shoot hand-held, never use filters other than a polarizer and any landscapes are always shot whilst "on the way" to some animal or another.

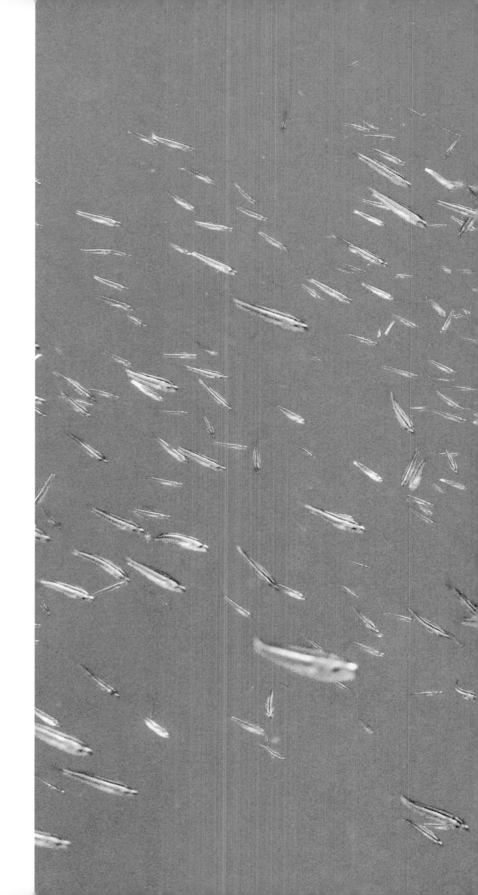

Galapagos green turtle

I simply love turtles. Whilst some purists will no doubt say that I should love all animals equally, I am human and, inevitably, certain animals trigger something within me that others do not. I had been with this particular turtle for quite some time, floating motionless above her as she fed, when she decided to come to the surface for air. This is always a busy time for me photographically, as it offers me the chance to get level with the turtle in clear blue water. However, this time a shoal of tiny fish swam in front of her and I immediately saw the Living Landscape unfold before me. The underwater world is a strangely silent one, but this image screams out to me the importance of protecting our oceans and keeping them pure for all to enjoy.

Marine iguana in habitat | Lava lizard on Galapagos sea lion
The connection on this page is one of scale. The image on the left shows a marine iguana in the context of the habitat that it calls home. In the distance is one of the volcanoes that ring the Galapagos and which were responsible for their birth and will ultimately be responsible for their death too. The image above also shows a reptile, a lava lizard, in its natural habitat, but in this case the habitat is another animal. Lava lizards seem to spend a fair amount of time in close proximity to sea lions and this lizard has crawled up onto the back of one. I watched as this lizard hunted for the flies that always seem to surround sea lions whenever they are out of the water. A good example of how the natural world works in harmony and where there is a synergy between two very different creatures.

Masked booby in water spray | Galapagos sea lion blowing bubbles

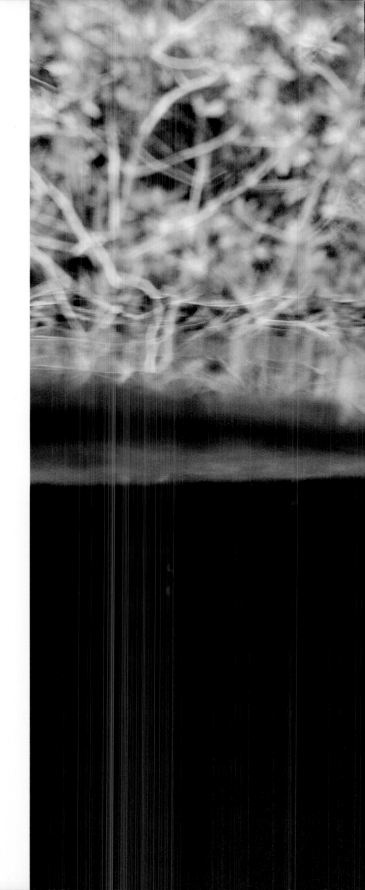

Galapagos green turtle in mangroves

A week before I took this image, I had been in this mangrove swamp and marvelled at the turtles swimming by underneath our boat. On my return visit I took my underwater camera housing as I was determined to record the turtles in a very different habitat from the norm. Very slowly, I placed the housing underwater and held it against the side of the boat to avoid spooking the turtles, as they came here to rest. I wanted to get a type of shot called an 'under-over' where you show the habitat above and below the water in the same frame. These shots are incredibly difficult to pull off, and it did not make things any easier that I was leaning over the side of a boat and unable to look into the viewfinder. Well, I don't think this is bad for my first attempt! From above the water looked clear, but underneath it was incredibly murky and this gives the turtle a ghost-like quality. I love this habitat shot as it really shows the Galapagos as the pristine unspoilt Eden that it is.

Masked booby chick on nest | Masked booby parent on nest

Magnificent frigate birds

Frigate birds follow every ship that sails around the Galapagos and, to me, they have always looked like harbingers of doom. Their silhouette is very prehistoric, pterodactyl-like in fact, and they look like remnants from a bygone age. I certainly felt like a photographer from a bygone age, too, sailing between islands, reclining on a sun lounger with a drink on one side and camera on the other. Sounds bliss, and it was; no wonder I found it so easy to see shots like this on that particular day.

Land iguana

It just takes one extra ingredient to turn a straight shot into something special. That extra ingredient is usually the light and in the minutes preceding this shot it had become very, very nice indeed. Unfortunately, the day was hot and the iguanas were leaving it late to come back to their burrows, so there was a good chance that one of the ingredients for my shot would be missing! Then, just as I thought all was lost, a lovely big male land iguana appeared from nowhere at the top of the track. I had two choices; move now and get the beautiful red light falling straight onto the iguana, or stay and gamble on a side-lit shot. Wildlife photography is always a gamble and I make big decisions all the time; usually they work, but not always. Always the gambler, I edged back down the path to give the iguana plenty of space to get into his burrow without being disturbed. Sure enough, he took the hint and came down the track towards me, picking up speed downhill all the time and throwing up dust in the process. It was a magical moment and one I was not going to miss.

Galapagos penguin diving | Galapagos green turtle ballet

The one shot I never managed to get for my penguin book was one underwater, and on Galapagos I actually swam with several. I stayed with this one for several minutes watching as he pushed out fish that were minding their own business underneath rocks and chased huge schools of fish. I watched the green turtle feeding too, although on algae. The ballet pose was caused by the incredibly strong current that buffeted both of us constantly, I had both fins wedged into rocks – something which my ankles would not let me forget for several days. Still art is nothing without a little sufferance!

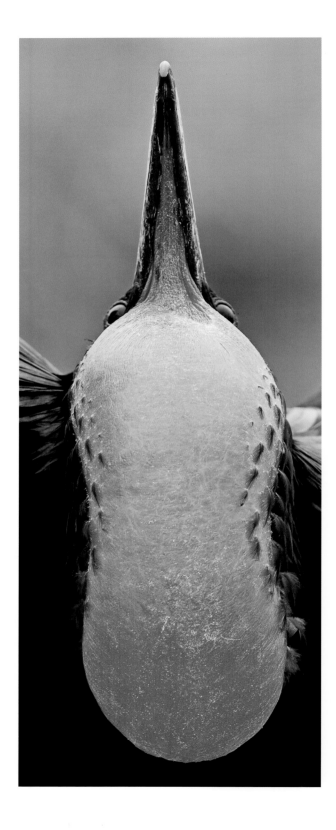

Magnificent frigate bird | Marine iguana at sunset

*Male magnificent frigate birds have an amazing red throat pouch that they inflate
to attract females onto their nest. When a female finally lands on the nest the male
raises his head up, which creates a very abstract image and a classic double take. The
iguana is an iconic image that just screams GALAPAGOS and nothing else really needs
to be said – less really is more.*

Marine iguana twosome | Masked booby twosome

Good things come in twos – or, to put it another way, just when you think that Galapagos has given you everything, it comes up with a couple of surprises on the final day. The first surprise was finding these two marine iguanas side by side, an imperfect pattern but a rarity in itself. The second was provided, not by the two masked boobies as there were plenty of those nesting all around, but by the light. I had suffered from disappointing light the whole trip and my opportunities for shooting anything evocative had been severely limited. Then, as I was dashing to get back to the ship, a shaft of light illuminated these two boobies on the track. It was a magical scene, as it looked and felt like I was on another planet: the incomparable and always inspirational Planet Galapagos.

THUMBNAILS

CAMERA GEAR AND EQUIPMENT

The images in this book were taken using either Canon (1DS MK2) or Nikon (D3, D300 and D700) cameras. I have been a Canon user for most of my career but changed to the Nikon system in December 2008 for the following reasons – high ISO performance, reliability and file quality. I have never looked back since and my creative photography has blossomed as a result of the flexibility that shooting at a high ISO gives me. I have also joined the fan club of the Nikon matrix metering system, as the days when I was prepared to spend time working out exposures are long past. For my fledgling underwater work, I use the D300 with a 20mm lens inside an Aquatech housing, but I may change systems this year to allow me to use my D700 with the 14-24mm lens; watch my BLOG for details.

My favourite lens is my Nikon 200-400mm zoom, closely followed by the 14-24mm super wide-angle zoom. Generally these follow me everywhere in my rucksack along with a 70-200mm f2.8 VR lens attached to a 1.4x teleconverter. I have a 600mm lens for use when the situation dictates, but always prefer using the 200-400 where possible as it allows me to compose my images and I can hold it without my arms falling off. I always work with two camera bodies, one attached to the wide-angle and one to a larger zoom, as that increases my flexibility and stops me wasting time changing lenses. I carry it all in my own custom-made rucksack, which I designed especially to cater for the needs of the serious working photographer.

All images are processed on my Mac Pro Workstation and edited when travelling on my MacBook Pro laptop. If I need to download in the field, I use the Jobo Giga Vu Pro Evolution and LaCie portable storage disks for backup. My monitor is a LaCie 519 LCD and is profiled using LaCie BlueEye software. All image processing uses a combination of software that includes Photo Mechanic, Adobe Camera Raw, Adobe Photoshop and various plug-ins. As new software is released, I constantly re-evaluate my workflow and make changes where necessary, so expect this list to change!

Clothing-wise, I wear Paramo Directional Clothing Systems as they are tough and keep out the elements. Together with Paramo, I have started the Aspira Fund, which is a way of using some of the profits from sales of the garments to help small conservation projects worldwide. This is a project close to my heart and one that I urge you to support. www.aspirafund.co.uk

Page 1
Roe buck at sunset
Roe deer (*Capreolus* capreolus)
UK

The result of patience and fieldcraft and nothing to do with any technical considerations whatsoever. Too much emphasis is placed on what gear we use as photographers and I hope that this book will redress the balance slightly to show that gear is irrelevant when you want to be creative.

Page 3
King penguin on beach
King penguin (*Aptenodytes patagonicus*)
Falkland Islands

I used the leading lines of the waves to balance the composition.

Page 5
Kingfisher in frost
European kingfisher (*Alcedo atthis*)
UK

An old image of mine taken when I was using film! To focus in tightly on the kingfisher would have been a waste of a wonderful frost and try as I might I have never managed to recreate this. Proof that you should make the most of every opportunity that presents itself.

Page 7
Lioness on windy day
African lion (*Panthera leo*)
Kenya

A traditional slide sandwich of two pictures merged together. I needed to use a shutter speed of 1/3rd second to blur the trees but try as I might I couldn't get the lion sharp at this speed. So I took a second image at 1/250th and combined the two. Although I do not like manipulation one bit, on this occasion the image is exactly faithful to the situation and is labelled as a digital composite. It is still, however, a cracking picture of a lion and, most importantly, is very different from the usual snoring portrait!

Page 8-9
King penguins on beach
King penguin (*Aptenodytes patagonicus*)
Falkland Islands

This is one of my favourite images of all time. For me, this has it all and clearly shows the benefit of including the habitat. It is far more than just a penguin image; it is a real Living Landscape.

Page 11
Lioness – if looks could kill
African lion (*Panthera leo*)
Zambia

An image that takes a second look and then you really see the menace in the eyes; I have no doubt that she was stalking me. Focus is a real problem with this kind of picture, as you need to be very precise with the composition to get a point right over the eye. I will remember that look for the rest of my life...

Page 12
Bengal tiger in temple
Bengal tiger (*Panthera tigris*)
India

Other photographers were taking this with 600mm lenses and 2x converters to try to fill the frame. Pointless. The story of the image is the temple and the tiger dwarfed inside it, so I deliberately used a 300mm lens and am aperture of f11 to get everything nicely sharp.

Page 14
Great grey owl chick
Great grey owl chick (*Strix nebulosa*)
Finland

I used a small amount of fill flash here to illuminate the owl against the bright sky. I am always careful with animals that have sensitive eyes so cut the power down by -3 stops and used a diffuser to ensure that the owl wasn't blinded by the light.

Page 15
Cheetahs and rainbow
Cheetah (*Acinonyx jubatus*)
Kenya

The shot here was definitely wide as the light level, despite the sun, was too low to contemplate using a long lens and getting anything sharp. So I used my 70-200mm to get a lovely habitat shot and the wide-angle approach hides the fact that the cheetahs are unimpressed by the rain and huddled up together.

Page 16-17
Starling murmuration
European starling (*Sturnus vulgaris*)
UK

One of the problems with these images is trying to get the starlings to show up clearly against the sky. I find that if I use a 70-200mm lens the compression is much better than with a 24-70mm and the starlings stand out better.

Page 18-19
Starling ballet
European starling (*Sturnus vulgaris*)
UK

Shooting with a wide-angle allows you to get the shapes which make the composition so compelling. Any natural pattern needs to be given space to breathe.

Page 20-21
Starling ballet
European starling (*Sturnus vulgaris*)
UK

I set an exposure compensation for -1 stop to ensure a good silhouette and generally set the ISO to 1000 to get a fast enough shutter speed to freeze the motion.

Page 22-23
Starling shapes
European starling (*Sturnus vulgaris*)
UK

Weather conditions are the key to a good murmuration; you need a nice sunny evening without much wind. Try to arrive at least 30 minutes before dusk as sometimes they turn up early!

Page 25
Arctic tern and iceberg
Arctic tern (*Sterna paradisaea*)
Svalbard

Since the message in this image is the scale, it was more important to get the tern in the correct position than to make sure that it was exactly sharp. Raising my ISO to 1000 on my D3, I shot at an aperture of f22 that ensured everything in the image would be sharp enough anyway.

Page 26
Grizzly on alert
Grizzly bear (*Ursus arctos*)
Alaska

I was caught out here by having a fixed 500mm lens to hand and nothing else. These days my 200-400 zoom would ensure that I gave the mountains a little more space, although it would be a very fine adjustment to ensure that the grizzly was not lost in the frame.

Page 27
Sally lightfoot crab and morning wave
Sally lightfoot crab (*Graspus adscensionis*)
Ascension Island

A rare use of my tripod; I kept the shutter speed to 1/30th second to blur the wave a little.

Page 28-29
Polar bear on blue ice
Polar bear (*Ursus maritimus*)
Canada

Whilst others in the tundra buggy shot this with a 500mm lens, I chose my 24-70mm instead, as the colour in the ice and sky was just incredible.

Page 30
Walrus sleeping
Atlantic walrus (*Odobenus rosmarus*)
Svalbard

I love dark and moody conditions for shots like these; somehow bright sunlight does not seem to tell the correct story.

Page 31
Crabeater seals on iceberg
Crabeater seal (*Lobodon carcinophagus*)
Antarctica

From the air, I prefer to use my 70-200 zoom lens rather than a fixed lens. Although I get less visible compression, the flexibility a zoom affords more than makes up for it.

Page 32-33
Rockhopper penguins and storm
Rockhopper penguin (*Eudyptes chrysocome*)
Falkland Islands

I am not precious about my camera gear as it is just a tool I use to express my creativity. Since I use it in all weathers, it generally spends its time inside Aquatech covers that allow me to shoot in any conditions.

Page 34-35
Red deer stag calling to hinds
Red deer (*Cervus elaphus*)
Scotland

Blasting away with a motor drive may sound good, but in situations like this, it gets you nowhere. I put the camera onto single-frame advance and took each shot very carefully, freezing immediately afterwards to gauge the deer's reaction. In fact during the whole of this encounter I took only two shots.

Page 36
Common wildebeest and cloud formation
Common wildebeest (*Connochaetes taurinus*)
Kenya

I love using cloud formations in my habitat images as I find them so much more appealing than just plain blue skies. Here I used a polarizer to give the image some much needed contrast and put the point of focus squarely on the centre of the herd.

Page 37
Bengal tiger on lake
Bengal tiger (*Panthera tigris*)
India

I used a 70-200mm lens so that I could use the trees to create a natural frame around this tiger.

Page 38-39
Gentoo penguins on Mars
Gentoo penguin (*Pygoscelis papua*)
Finland

Timing is everything. I waited several days to get the light right for this image, as I knew that it had to be something special to lift the starkness out of the habitat.

Page 40-41
Wildebeest herd and approaching storms
Common wildebeest (*Connochaetes taurinus*)
Kenya

At first glance, this looks like a pretty boring shot but it tells the big story of why the wildebeest migrate. In the foreground, there are wildebeest grazing on fresh grass whilst on the horizon there are storms bringing the rain that triggers new growth of the grass. Sometimes a subtle image can tell the best story.

Page 42
Grey seal at sunset
Grey seal (*Salichoerus grypus*)
UK

One of the worst problems that still occur with a DSLR is the burnout of the sun's disc. Usually I would not even have attempted this shot, but on this day it was slightly misty which dulled it enough to give a quite interesting effect. I would never consider manipulating an image to add a "new sun"; it just doesn't seem to be ethical to me.

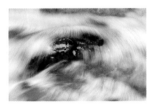

Page 43
Sally lightfoot crab
Sally lightfoot crab (*Graspus adscensionis*)
Ascension Island

There were many crabs filter feeding on the rocks, so I watched how the waves broke over each and chose the one that looked the best. Shutter speed was around 1/3rd second; the main problem was keeping the tripod still in the waves. I solved this by hanging a huge bag of rocks from it.

Page 44-45
Knot roost
Knot (*Calidris canuta*)
UK

The soft morning light meant that no filters were needed for this, as the sky was not so bright. An aperture of f16 ensured that I had enough foreground to background detail. Since I was handholding the 14-24mm zoom, I increased the ISO to 1250, to keep the shutter speed up.

Page 46
Green turtle hatching
Green turtle (*Chelonia mydas*)
Ascension Island

I shot this image with a wide-angle lens to deliberately make the hatchling look dwarfed by the habitat and the sea behind it.

Page 47
Grizzly on Katmai coast
Grizzly bear (*Ursus arctos*)
Alaska

There is nothing technically skilful about the image; it is shot just the way I saw it and anyone could have done the same in the same situation. Sometimes pictures do not need to be created, they are there for all to see.

Page 48-49
Wildebeest walking on tracks
Common wildebeest (*Connochaetes taurinus*)
Kenya

I deliberately composed this image to give space to the two groups of wildebeest and to show the stark habitat through which they migrate. I was glad of the harsh midday light as it adds to the feel of the shot.

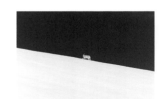

Page 50
Mountain hare running
Mountain hare (*Lepus timidus*)
UK

Exposure in these conditions is always difficult, so I spot metered from the snow and compensated by +2 stops.

Page 51
Polar bear in snowstorm
Polar bear (*Ursus maritimus*)
Svalbard

It was about minus 40 when I took this and seconds later my lens and camera froze up completely.

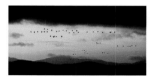

Page 52-53
Barnacle geese formations
Barnacle goose (*Branta leucopsis*)
Scotland

This is the result of several days' field craft trying to find out their regular flyways from the roost sites to the feeding grounds. Proof that technical skill is useless without an appreciation of the wildlife that you are working with and that good wildlife photography cannot be rushed.

Page 54-55
Wildebeest herd in rain
Common wildebeest (*Connochaetes taurinus*)
Kenya

I never worry about my lens in the rain as it can deal with it and I would rather get the shot and not be precious about it. The camera, however, is another matter; it has zero tolerance for serious rain and must always be covered.

Page 56
European brown bear in forest
European brown bear (*Ursus arctos*)
Finland

Preparation was the key and I had three lenses sticking out from the hide ready to shoot – a wide-angle, a short zoom and a long telephoto. For this image, I chose the wide-angle as I love the patterns of the pines.

Page 57
Mountain gorillas relaxing
Mountain gorilla (*Gorilla beringei*)
Rwanda

Shooting gorillas wide-angle is never easy as the sky is generally quite bland and several stops different from the gorilla. I could have used an ND filter to balance the sky but in these conditions it is impractical so I opted for a safe exposure that ensured the highlights were not blown out at the expense of some dark shadows. That is what software is designed to fix!

Page 58-59
Namaqua chameleon in desert
Namaqua chameleon (*Chamaeleo namaquensis*)
Namibia

The harsh light was a real problem here so I used a circular polarizing filter on my medium-format camera lens.

Page 60-61
Greater flamingos feeding
Greater flamingo (*Phoenicopterus roseus*)
Kenya

Getting this image was a question of striking a balance between getting a decent depth of field and having enough speed to stop the motion of the flamingos flying across. I chose an aperture of f11, shooting at 1/250th sec.

Page 62-63
Gentoo penguin stretching
Gentoo penguin (*Pygoscelis papua*)
Antarctica

When I am working from a small boat I always increase the ISO and decrease the aperture so that I can get the best possible shutter speed. In my experience having a shutter speed that is too slow ruins these types of pictures, as boats tend to wobble around too much.

Page 64-65
Snow geese blast-off
Snow goose (*Chen caerulescens*)
USA

To get such a slow shutter speed, 1/13th second, would usually mean having a large aperture and therefore depth of field. Although I wanted the geese to be in focus, I did not want the background to be in focus as it would be distracting. Increasing the ISO allowed me to get the aperture I needed.

Page 66
Snow geese festival
Snow goose (*Chen caerulescens*) and people
USA

Taking pictures of wildlife is wonderful, but sometimes you can generate a more powerful message by including people actually watching wildlife in the picture – but remember to ask their permission first. This was taken during the annual Festival of the Snow Goose in New Mexico.

Page 67
Snow geese
Snow goose (*Chen caerulescens*)
USA

I deliberately under-exposed this image to bring out the intense colours but also to ensure that the whites of the geese were not blown out.

Page 68-69
Snow geese mountain sunrise
Snow goose (*Chen caerulescens*)
USA

Digital SLRs are incredible at picking up detail in low light. I could barely see with my eyes here, but at ISO 800, the camera did a great job. Since the exposure was quite long at 25 seconds, I used the camera's in-built noise-reduction and locked up the mirror before exposure to reduce any vibration.

Page 70-71
Afternoon clouds over feeding snow geese
Snow goose (*Chen caerulescens*)
USA

Living Landscapes with a clear, featureless blue sky can be very dull and I always look for interesting cloud formations to give the picture that extra special something.

Page 72-73
Snow geese landing
Snow goose (*Chen caerulescens*)
USA

If you are unsure about letting your creative side loose, take your normal shots first so you can relax in the knowledge that you have something to be proud of 'in the can'. Then, take something that pushes your boundaries. If it does not work, figure out why and try it slightly differently next time.

Page 74
Snow geese patterns
Snow goose (*Chen caerulescens*)
USA

This image was taken with a 70-200mm lens, which is proof that you do not always need a big lens for wildlife photography. I find that a long lens limits you to one kind of shot – usually a close-up, which may not be the best story to tell at that time.

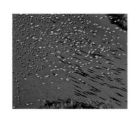

Page 75
Snow geese aerial
Snow goose (*Chen caerulescens*)
USA

Every day, photography is a learning curve and on this particular day I learnt to have two cameras with me at all times. For some reason, I only took one up in the plane with me and missed the better wide-angle shot here because I only had the 70-200mm lens attached. Now I never go anywhere without two cameras and as a result I think that my creativity has improved.

Page 76-77
Snow geese close up
Snow goose (*Chen caerulescens*)
USA

Sometimes even the biggest lens will not get you close enough; so here I used my 400mm lens and cropped the resulting image. Since the image is not intended to be sharp, it can then be interpolated to any size that I want, even billboard. Sharpness is irrelevant with this image and what a refreshing change that makes!

Page 78-79
Snow geese abstract
Snow goose (*Chen caerulescens*)
USA

Yes, I know, totally weird shapes. When I took this with a high shutter speed, the cottonwoods behind were just too distracting for the composition. So I slowed the speed down, let the geese move through the frame and the background now blends with the artistic feel of the geese taking off.

Page 80-81
Snow geese and paper airplanes
Snow goose (*Chen caerulescens*)
USA

The point of focus here is right in the middle of the lake as I knew the large aperture I was using would bring the mountains into sharp focus. To help the colour of the sky and water, I put on my beard and used a circular polarizer.

Page 82-83
Snow geese taking off from lake
Snow goose (*Chen caerulescens*)
USA

A very difficult shot to execute, as there was no way that the autofocus points at the edge of the viewfinder would be accurate enough to keep focus on the flying geese. Since they were flying towards me, I focused on a point halfway between the group of geese and my car and used an aperture of f11 to get enough depth of field with my 70-200mm lens. Sometimes common sense overrules technology.

Page 84-85
Snow geese rowing
Snow goose (*Chen caerulescens*)
USA

These geese look like they are rowing, which produces an incredible pattern in the sky. Again this is a good example of how being creative can yield some amazing results which you could not achieve any other way.

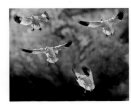

Page 86
Snow geese landing
Snow goose (*Chen caerulescens*)
USA

When faced with a group of birds landing, I always pick one near the centre of the shot where the autofocus is most accurate. I keep tracking this one bird all the way into landing and ignore all the others around it.

Page 87
Geese at sunrise
Snow goose (*Chen caerulescens*)
USA

A silhouette should be a silhouette, so I always underexpose by at least 1 stop to ensure that there is no detail in the subject.

Page 88-89
Painting with snow geese
Snow goose (*Chen caerulescens*)
USA

I cannot give you any hard and fast rule here, as it is pure experimentation and creativity. Or to put another way, it is just fun.

Page 90
Snow geese head-on
Snow goose (*Chen caerulescens*)
USA

The technique here is again to pick a single bird near the centre, lock on to it and follow it for the first few seconds of flight. Provided you have a steady hand, the autofocus should be able to lock on to the bird and not the background!

Page 91
Snow geese at sunset
Snow goose (*Chen caerulescens*)
USA

The beautiful colours of the sunset combine well with the white tones of the geese to make this really atmospheric shot. It is always tempting to focus in tightly on the geese but they need space to fly into for the composition to work.

Page 92-93
A rolling wave of snow geese
Snow goose (*Chen caerulescens*)
USA

Sometimes it pays to just put the camera down, stand back and smile at nature in all its glory.

Page 95
Starling ball
European starling (*Sturnus vulgaris*)
UK

I compensated the camera to -1 1/3rd stops to ensure that all of the starlings were in silhouette. I decided to freeze the motion as I had previously tried to let it flow a bit without any success, so selected an ISO of 1600 on my Nikon D3 to get a decent shutter speed.

Page 96
Starlings over canal
European starling (*Sturnus vulgaris*)
UK

One reason I always carry two identical Nikon D3's now is so that one can have a wide-angle lens attached and one can have a decent zoom. This allows me to react to all situations and shoot wide when I get the chance without having to dive for my rucksack. In this case it was the wide-angle.

Page 97
Marine iguana landscape
Marine iguana (*Amblyrhynchus cristatus*)
Galapagos

I love the effect of a 14mm lens on a full frame DSLR as it gives a stunning super-wide-angle feel without too much distortion. It is important to get everything sharp from the foreground to the background, so either work out your hyper-focal distance or just cheat and set the aperture to f22.

Page 98-99
Land iguana eye
Land iguana (*Conolophus subcristatus*)
Galapagos

The composition works here because the eye is offset and the shallow depth of field draws all attention to it. There is no rule that states everything has to be central when taking abstracts – it depends on the individual shot and what you think works best.

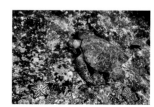

Page 100-101
Galapagos green turtle and sea stars
Galapagos green turtle (*Chelonia mydas agassisi*)
Galapagos

One reason I will never be a dive photographer is that I flatly refuse to use flash underwater. In fact, I hate flash, full stop, and it would have ruined the feeling of this image, too. Like most of my photography, this uses natural light and is all the better for it.

Page 102-103
King penguin colony from the air
King penguin (*Aptenodytes patagonicus*)
South Georgia

This is one of my favourite pattern images. It was taken from 2000 feet and the brown shapes are juvenile penguins in a crèche whilst every other shape is an adult penguin. When looking straight down like this, the aperture needs to be only f5.6-f8 as it is the shutter speed that needs to be kept very high. Compositionally I let you all off a bit by including the grass to give some scale...

Page 104-105
Wildbeest herd in motion
Common wildebeest (*Connochaetes taurinus*)
Kenya

To get this image, I set up my 70-200mm zoom on top of the vehicle supported by a beanbag and used a two-second exposure to get the movement. Since this is a more creative image, there is no need to worry about the sharpness of an individual animal as it is the impression of movement that counts.

Page 106-107
Walrus whiskers
Atlantic walrus (*Odobenus rosmarus*)
Svalbard

Ideally, I should have shot this with a much greater depth of field, as I only used f8. A better choice would have been f16 and to stand slightly higher, to get more of the whiskers sharp. However, I had to put the welfare of the walrus first and to stand higher might have scared it off; the wrong choice of aperture, though, was purely my mistake and it will not be the last I make.

Page 108-109
African elephant abstract
African elephant (*Loxodonta africana*)
Botswana

The ears pretty much give it away and I debated for a long time whether to include the eye. However, if I had it would have turned the attention away from the light and the texture of the skin, so I decided to crop the eye out and make this a more traditional pattern image.

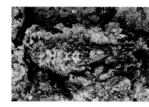

Page 110
Stonefish camouflage
Reef stonefish (*Synanceia horrida*)
Galapagos

I was forced to shoot this a lot tighter than I wanted to as it was sitting close to the surface. My primary concern was to keep my legs away from those spines as the water was pretty rough. It was one time when a zoom inside my underwater housing would have been a blessing.

Page 111
Wildebeest at waterhole
Common wildebeest (*Connochaetes taurinus*)
Kenya

Nothing award winning for me to do here apart from getting the picture in focus. The light was unhelpful, though, as it was pretty harsh. Luckily the pattern of the waterhole made up for any aesthetic inadequacies!

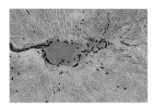

Page 112-113
Leopard shadow
Species African leopard (*Panthera pardus*)
South Africa

I am not suggesting for one minute that when you have a chance to take a perfect shot of a leopard you should just ignore it and look for something abstract. When the situation is good, then take all the shots you can, as it will be a rare encounter. All I am trying to say is that when the situation isn't good (in this case it was right into the bright setting sun) then don't immediately give up and look for another option.

Page 114-115
Wildebeest shadows
Common wildebeest (*Connochaetes taurinus*)
Kenya

Shadows make excellent patterns, especially if they are strong, bold shapes that are easily recognized. This image would work equally well with giraffe or elephants, for example; but with animals such as gazelles the shadows are just too indistinct.

Page 116
Land iguana skin
Land iguana (*Conolophus subcristatus*)
Galapagos

I prefer to take shots like this with natural light rather than flash, as I feel that the colours and tones are subtler and more like I see them with my naked eye.

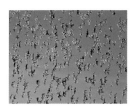

Page 117
Knot flock flying
Knot (*Calidris canuta*)
UK

Rather than taking a wide-angle shot of the whole flock, I decided to zoom in a little and show individual birds. I did this not only because they were all banking at the same time, but also because of the winter light on them, which was simply stunning.

Page 118-119
Knot flock
Knot (*Calidris canuta*)
UK

Shots like this are one of the few occasions that I use a tripod, as I want the motion to be horizontal and not vertical. The light level was appalling as it was raining, but it didn't matter as I wanted a slow speed so I reduced the ISO from my usual 1000 to 400 to give the exposure a couple of stops of extra blur.

Page 120-121
Land iguana close-up
Land iguana (*Conolophus subcristatus*)
Galapagos

I would have preferred to have a little more habitat in this shot, but it distracted attention from the iguana so I cropped it out. The light was just incredible and the image was taken with my 200-400mm lens at an aperture of f4 @ ISO 1000.

Page 122
Marine iguana with friendly lava lizard
Marine iguana (*Amblyrhynchus cristatus*)
Galapagos

The light was really awful as we had landed late after a rough overnight crossing and it was close to midday. I used a circular polarizer to cut down the harsh shadows, but only by a little. Polarizers can be over-used and it is important to retain an element of reality in the final shot.

Page 123
Volcanic habitat
Galapagos

Although I am not a natural landscape photographer I really enjoy it and have worked hard to get my technique up to scratch. A combination of my propensity for handholding and the need for an aperture of f22 means that I generally use a much higher ISO than most landscape photographers ever would. Now that I use the Nikon D3 this is not a problem and this image was shot at an ISO of 1000, whilst still retaining an amazing image quality.

Page 124-125
Red cardinal shoal
Red cardinal (*Apogon quadrisquamatus*)
Galapagos

These red cardinals are tiny, about the size of your thumb, but what they lack in size, they make up for by shoaling in thousands. These shoals were in the shadow of a large overhanging rock, so the shutter speed was well down. Unfortunately I could not do much about it with my housing, hence the slight amount of blur.

Page 126-127
Galapagos green turtle
Galapagos green turtle (*Chelonia mydas agassisi*)
Galapagos

Getting so much in focus for an aperture of f8 is the reason I only use a wide-angle lens in my housing. I am not yet good enough underwater to cope with working a zoom lens – it is quite stressful enough trying to see through a viewfinder with a mask in the way.

Page 128
Marine iguana in habitat
Marine iguana (*Amblyrhynchus cristatus*)
Galapagos

Again I used a polarizer here to cut down the reflections on the water. The light conditions were overcast with a hint of sun that gave the water an unflattering cast. I knew that, to make the landscape work, I needed some detail in the back of the pool. I set f16 to ensure a decent depth of field and ISO 800 to keep the shutter speed nice and high.

Page 129
Lava lizard on sea lion
Lava lizard (*Tropidurus*)
Galapagos

Nothing exceptional about this shot. I deliberately kept in the edges of the sea lion to give scale, as well as a clue to what you are looking at!

Page 130
Masked booby in water spray
Masked booby (*Sula dactylatra*)
Galapagos

A real double-take shot. This booby was flying through the spray generated from a blowhole on the island of Espaniola. I had watched the blowhole for ages but had struggled to make any sense of it photographically until the booby came along. It works because it is unusual and so different from the 50 million static masked booby images that I already have. Being different is cool.

Page 131
Galapagos sea lion blowing bubbles
Galapagos sea lion (*Zalophus wollebaeki*)
Galapagos

Timing and the ability to predict animal behaviour are the critical factors in wildlife photography, not what gear you have. I had already watched this sea lion surface and blow out bubbles many times, so when it headed for the surface again I kicked upwards and waited for the moment to come. After that it was just a matter of timing and remembering to breathe.

Page 132-133
Galapagos green turtle in mangroves
Galapagos green turtle (*Chelonia mydas agassisi*)
Galapagos

Before immersing the housing in the water, I selected the autofocus point at the bottom of the viewfinder. I hoped that this would ensure that the turtle was in sharp focus and that the aperture of f8 would get some of the habitat, too. Then it was just down to guesswork and concentration as I was determined to get the shot for my Galapagos portfolio.

Page 134
Masked booby chick on nest
Masked booby (*Sula dactylatra*)
Galapagos

This is one of a series of shots I took with a variety of lenses showing a very chilled out youngster on the nest. I like this one particularly as it fits in with the ethos of this book. At first you are not sure what you are looking at and need to take a second glance, but then the amazing eye really stands out. To get the low depth of field, I used my 200-400mm lens at 400mm and a low aperture of f4.

Page 135
Masked booby on nest
Masked booby (*Sula dactylatra*)
Galapagos

This image has a different sense of scale from the others; it was taken with a 14mm lens to accentuate the habitat. The masked booby was unable to move from her lava nest due to the constant attention of egg-loving predators, so she had made a sundial of her necessities. I liked the effect of this, so stood up high to get her in the foreground with the lava habitat leading off to the sea.

Page 136-137
Magnificent frigate birds
Magnificent frigate bird (*Fregata magnificens*)
Galapagos

It was midday and the sky was brighter than you see here, so I used -2 stops in compensation to increase the mood and dramatic effect. Then I just lay on my back, looked through the viewfinder and waited for a pattern to form.

Page 138-139
Land iguana
Land iguana (*Conolophus subcristatus*)
Galapagos

Since the light was getting low, I had previously dialled in ISO 1600 and, boy, was I glad that I had. Anything less and this shot would have been a blur, which might actually have worked in a different way but it was not the shot I wanted. When the iguana started moving, I kept the autofocus point right over the face and picked my images carefully as I did not want to run out of memory buffer.

Page 140
Galapagos penguin diving
Galapagos penguin (*Spheniscus mendiculus*)
Galapagos

A difficult shot to get and more of a 'point and hope' than anything planned, but, as I have said throughout this book, it is better to try and miss than not try at all.

Page 141
Galapagos green turtle ballet
Galapagos green turtle (*Chelonia mydas agassisi*)
Galapagos

This is an unusual shot that adds to the diversity of my turtle portfolio and gives more insight into turtle life than a picture of one swimming in blue water. I have always said that a portfolio containing a body of work on one species can say far more about a photographer than individual shots.

Page 142
Magnificent frigate bird throat pouch
Magnificent frigate bird (*Fregata magnificens*)
Galapagos

The problem with frigate birds is that the habitat can be quite distracting, which takes the focus away from the pouch. So I used my 200-400mm lens to get in close and then cropped the image in Photoshop to a vertical window format.

Page 143
Marine iguana at sunset
Marine iguana (*Amblyrhynchus cristatus*)
Galapagos

I watched the iguanas for some time and worked out that they were walking off the beach to a lagoon via this sand dune. Lying down behind it put the ridge straight ahead of me against the setting sun that would give a perfect silhouette. All I had to do was to wait for a willing iguana and set the camera to -2 stops compensation to ensure a silhouette

Page 144
Marine iguana twosome
Marine iguana (*Amblyrhynchus cristatus*)
Galapagos

One of the rare times when I would have used a macro lens, but being a complete muppet with them, I do not own one. Instead I used a 24-70mm and shot straight down with an aperture of f8 to ensure all was nice and sharp.

Page 145
Masked booby twosome
Masked booby (*Sula dactylatra*)
Galapagos

Worrying about exposure would have ruined this shot as I literally had seconds to get it, so I just trusted the Nikon matrix meter on the D3 and gave it +1/3rd stop compensation as I was shooting into the light. Compositionally speaking, the horizon unfortunately cuts across the back of the boobies. In this case I felt it was justified, as I wanted the habitat behind to be included. Remember, this is not a record shot but a Living Landscape. That means my own rules apply and they are very simple: there aren't any.

Back cover image
Dancing lemur
Verreaux's sifaka lemur (*Propithecus verreauxi*)
Madascar

Sometimes all the preparation in the world means nothing, you just have to shoot and hope!

THANKS

I would like to thank the following people for their help and assistance with *Living Landscapes:*

PVV, Colin McCarthy, Gabrielle Nowak, John Njenga, Commodore Nick Lambert RN, Ian & Marion Moncrieff, Stimpy, Mike, Eggy, Simon, Pete, Rowly and all the crew of HMS *Endurance*, Aditya and Poonam Singh, Salim Ali, Shailin and Rhea Ramji, Andrew Jackson, Arne Kristoffersen, Brad Josephs, Steve Banner, Will Bolsover, Artie Morris, Carol Tang, Robert O'Toole, Rich and Dawn Steel, Per and the crew of M/S *Stockholm*, Tim Harris, Lee Dalton, Steve and Alison Kaluski, Jeremy Gilbert, James Banfield, Dave Glanfield from camerasunderwater.co.uk, Will Bolsover, John and Moussa, James Lees, Tracey Rich, Donald and Sheena, Gordon Robertson, Andrew Momberg, Nigel Lewis and Ian Salisbury. My thanks also go out to everyone who has travelled with me in the past few years, I hope that you have been inspired and continue to love the world around us. My clients also get my heartfelt thanks; your continued support helps me realise all of my dreams.

Special thanks must go to Piers, Bill and all at Aurum Press for their belief in my vision and to designer and mentor extraordinaire Eddie Ephraums, without whom this project would never have made it out of my head.

My website www.andyrouse.co.uk has a very popular BLOG, an online library with 10,000 keyworded images and details of my expeditions and events. Please drop by and take a look!